BURN HILL

BURN HILL

Growing Up Dirt Poor and Hilariously Rich

by

Andrew Louis Hale

Distributed by Skinny Brown Dog Media

Interior and cover design by Skinny Brown Dog Media

Editing Support Courtney Oppel

Library of Congress Cataloging-in-Publication Data

ISBN 978-1-957506-64-7 (paperback)

ISBN 978-1-957506-67-8 (ebook)

ISBN 978-1-957506-65-4 (hardcover)

ISBN 978-1-957506-66-1 (case laminate)

DEDICATION

I dedicate this book to my beloved wife, Virginia, who patiently assisted me in typing and retyping several of the initial chapters from my clumsily handwritten notes, during a time when home computers were not yet commonplace.

Additionally, I dedicate this book to my two children, Cheryl and Justin, as well as to my grandchildren, Danielle, Andrew, Quinn, Austin, Amanda, Jude, and Tessa. Furthermore, I extend this dedication to my great-grandchildren, Daxton, Isla, Sophia, and all those who will come after. You are profoundly cherished and have been the wellspring of inspiration for this book.

CONTENTS

WHY I WROTE THIS BOOK

I am not an author, but I wrote a book.

I grew up dirt poor in the 1950's in a place called Burn Hill, near the small town of Arlington, in rural Washington State. Life was simple and profoundly primitive, yet eight kids made sure life was filled with adventure and hilarity. What we lacked in material prosperity we made up for in the riches of family, homespun entertainment, and adventure. The short stories I write in this book are true and intended to bring a smile to your face.

I did not write this book because I have a passion for writing, or because I felt a need to promote myself. I wrote because I was compelled to preserve a family history that could only be done through words on paper. I wrote because I want my kids, grandkids, great grandkids, and those that follow to know that a wonderful life does not require material wealth. Additionally, I wrote to honor the memory of my remarkable parents.

I don't write about poverty or hardships, as if those things defined my childhood, nor will I bore you with stories about grandma's cherry pie, or that walking to school was uphill both ways. I choose rather to write about the hilarious adventures I experienced as a young country boy.

You may not desire or choose a Burn Hill experience for yourself, but if you ever find yourself without material wealth, make sure you grasp the grander pursuits of life – "Faith, Hope and Love." Choose confidence over worry, wisdom over status, friendship over possessions and find joy through faith and family.

If Burn Hill inspires you to write your own story, it will be one the greatest accomplishments of your life and a cherished gift to your descendants.

"Life does not consist in an abundance of possessions." Luke 12:15

Andrew Louis Hale

INTRODUCTION

The roots of my childhood run deep into the hardpan soil of a small farm located three miles southeast of the town of Arlington in Washington State. The old farm on Burn Hill remains vivid in my memory as a solid rock. It was a country-boy utopia, the embodiment of adventure at its best.

An orchard graced the grassy hillside, a creek wound through fields of timothy grass, and a humble wooden frame house stood amidst various outbuildings. Beyond the barn, a vast wood beckoned. This farm wasn't a fancy dude ranch, but it was country, and country was living.

On March 17, 1945, exactly a year and a day before my birth, my parents, Donald and Dorothy Hale, affectionately known as Pa and Ma, moved their small and growing family onto the farm. The primitive farmhouse had a front door and a back door, but little else. Even the most basic essentials were lacking. There was no foundation, no insulation, no electricity, no indoor plumbing, and no bathroom. Firewood fueled the cookstove and living room heater, kerosene powered the lamps, and ice kept the "fridge" cool. The washing machine was not found inside the house, but outdoors, as it was powered by a gasoline motor.

Improvements to the house had to be made without outside help, using used materials. Some of these improvements would take years to complete, while others would never come to fruition.

To say that this was a hardship and struggle for Pa and Ma would be an understatement. However, their dedication to the task at hand, Ma's willingness to do without and improvise, their strength, their commitment to each other and us kids, and their dependence on God Almighty are etched in Heaven.

Although Pa and Ma carefully named each of their eight children born into their home, David and Odin, the two eldest, just as carefully renamed each one. Priscilla, the third born, was renamed Annie Oakley. Marilyn was labeled Mutt. As the fifth born, I reluctantly assumed the name Cramp. Reuben, the sixth born, eventually became known as Batis. Stephen went by the handle Dezeets or Dez, and Sharon, the eighth born, was appropriately renamed Bits.

The farm was not entirely self-supporting, but it did contribute significantly to what graced our kitchen table. Cows, goats, sheep, pigs, rabbits, chickens, ducks, geese, and a bountiful vegetable garden all contributed to the menu.

The Hale farm was a place of hard work but also a place of spirited adventures and hilarious times. There were times of solitude and times of lively chaos. The farm may have been financially modest, but we were blessed in countless ways.

The events chronicled in this book are true and are written from my memories of life on Burn Hill. While the stories are true, I use my imagination to relive these events and include the kinds of conversations, humor, sarcasm, and banter that were always present in the Hale family. I do not focus solely on poverty, hardships, or struggles as if they were the only defining aspects of our lives. Instead, I write about the richness, adventure, and hilarity I experienced as a young country boy, as well as the humor I now find looking back. Remembering how it was brings a smile to my face and gratitude to my heart.

When I began to write, I had no intention of writing a book. I initially wrote a story called "The Bull" as a bedtime story to read to my two kids, Cheryl and Justin, when they were five and six years old. After writing that story, I started considering the possibility of compiling a book of stories from my childhood. I was never much of an academic, nor did I have a great interest in books, so the thought of writing a book seemed like a daunting task. The writing of this book took over forty-five years. I wrote in spurts, with long stretches of time when I wrote nothing and other times when I was able to produce a couple of chapters within a week. I am not proud of my slowness, but I am deeply satisfied that through this book, I am keeping alive the stories of Burn Hill.

Andrew Louis Hale

(Andy) aka Cramp

CHAPTER ONE

———— •+• ————

ANIMAL CONTROL

The Hale farm encompassed ten acres and housed a remarkable assortment of animals—a veritable zoo that showcased the intricate balance of ecology, where humans and critters coexisted, sometimes even harmoniously. This delicate equilibrium was no accident but the result of a careful orchestration by every member of the Hale family.

Among the various responsibilities of farm life, animal control took the lead as the most challenging and undoubtedly the most fascinating. It certainly held more appeal than tasks such as liming the outhouse, stacking firewood, or weeding the rutabaga patch.

To someone unfamiliar with farm life, animal control might conjure up images of a young boy herding cows up a winding path to the barn for evening milking. However, that notion is pure fantasy. Getting our solitary cow into the barn took more than just a small boy; it was primarily Pa's responsibility, with my older brother Odin occasionally lending a hand.

On some occasions, Odin would return from a milking session with an empty bucket. It appeared Bossie, our clever cow, had developed a mischievous game. She must have learned it during her time at the Entsminger farm before we acquired her. Perhaps that explains why Mr. Entsminger, a farmer from Edgecomb, sold Bossie at a bargain price.

The rules of this cow game vary from farm to farm, but the objective remains the same. First, the cow will locate the nearly full bucket of milk, typically nestled between the milker's knees beneath the aft end of the cow's underbelly. The cow will find this bucket using either its right or left hoof, demonstrating a remarkable skill to do so without looking, as that would alert the vigilant milker. Second, the cow will become entirely awkward—a feat that comes naturally to cows. Before the milker can react, the cow will kick the bucket to the other side of the barn. For extra points, the cow will send the milker and their stool flying as well.

Cows exhibit little concern and show absolutely no emotion when the bucket and/or milker are sent flying. Even if you yell something like "You ignorant Holstein!" the cow will interpret it as "The milking session is now over; you may exit to your left." When verbalizing proves ineffective, the milker might resort to physical confrontations. After a few well-placed punches to the side of the critter, a cow will respond with complete apathy.

While cows possess a particular kind of personality, goats seemed to come from another planet. Unlike the gentle and peaceful sheep, goats are belligerent and cocky. The goats, whose names must be omitted from this account, were large, pushy, and ornery creatures who attempted to assert their dominance over Ma. Whenever Ma dumped a panful of vegetable peelings to feed the ducks and chickens, the goats would barge in. Ma took the side of her feathered friends and pounded the heads of these billies with her pan. Whether the goats benefited intellectually from the pounding is doubtful, but the pans certainly took on new shapes.

One of our goats made it his mission to observe us during supper. No, we didn't invite him as an official spectator; he simply leaped onto the outside window ledge. Perched precariously on the narrow ledge, Mr. Goat would stare as humans ate, watching each forkful of potatoes and gravy make its way from the dinner plate to the mouth. Ma didn't appreciate this intrusion, but we kids paid little attention as we were more concerned with who was forking the last piece of fried chicken.

It would be an understatement to say that goats love to climb on top of things. Besides window ledges, you could expect to find them on woodpiles, shed roofs, and farm equipment. When the goats started eyeing the automobiles, we knew we had to find a way to keep these adventurous climbers on the ground.

No one was more concerned than Dave, who had recently purchased a beautiful 1951 Chevy hardtop. With the goats eyeing this sleek beauty, Dave set out to solve the animal control predicament.

One Sunday morning, after securing each goat to a log with a chain, we left for meeting in Dave's new car (we referred to church gatherings as "meetings"). Undoubtedly, Dave felt satisfied with his animal control solution, as there was no mention of goats either on the way to the meeting or on the return journey. However, as we turned into the driveway, some of the kids began shouting about a goat.

"What goat?" demanded Dave.

"That goat right there!" said Pa.

What Dave and Pa faced was a significant problem: animal control gone awry, and goats going predictable. There in the orchard, under the shade of a cherry tree, sat Pa's Chevy sedan with a goat standing triumphantly on its top yet still attached to the log by a chain.

No farm would be complete without a trusty dog. A good dog is invaluable for protecting against unwanted intruders and animals and is regarded as man's best friend.

Queenie, our beloved dog, was part German Shepherd, part something else, and part chicken. The chicken characteristics were most evident when someone yelled "sic 'em!" Queenie would take off after the intruder like a fierce junkyard dog, only to stop a few feet away and wag her tail, inviting the intruder to join us for supper.

This overly friendly behavior toward strangers and intruders became an irritant to the Hale family, especially when her friendliness extended to male dogs. Birth control, a delicate subject for some, became part of our animal control responsibilities. We kids willingly assumed this duty and fulfilled it with vigilance and crude efficiency. When the season was right, all the dogs from town, located three miles away, would arrive. It was the most motley crew of scraggly mongrels and hounds you could ever imagine. These town dogs had no regard for private property, law and order, or common decency. Since Queenie wouldn't keep them off the farm, we took measures to make their visits memorable and miserable.

I believe it was Odin who excelled in this aspect of animal control. One unfortunate mongrel found himself trapped in a fifty-five-gallon barrel while Odin pelted him with rocks and firecrackers. This likely resulted in a severe loss of memory, as the moment the mongrel was released from the barrel, he forgot why he had come to the farm and promptly returned to town. Priscilla (or Annie Oakley, as she was often called) wanted no part in animal control. "You kids don't understand these things; and besides, your behavior is barbaric," she would say. She always seemed to say things that sounded important but didn't make much sense.

Protecting Queenie from these stray dogs became a twenty-four-hour job, requiring her to be brought into the house at night. However, there was still the issue of the dogs outside, fighting and causing a ruckus. One particularly hilarious night, a scruffy-haired mongrel circled the house incessantly. We kids faithfully carried out our assumed duties from an upstairs bedroom window. Armed with ammunition, we attempted to convince this shaggy intruder that he was unwelcome on the farm. Our ammunition for the night consisted of chunks of firewood that we quickly gathered upstairs while Ma and Pa weren't watching.

This intruder dog was obviously a dedicated canine and a brute for punishment, for each time he circled beneath our window he was bombarded with firewood. Like a zombie on night watch, he rounded the house, passing below our bomb-bay window once every couple of minutes. With Mutt and I sitting in the open window, and with Batis and Dez eagerly waiting their turn, we happily fulfilled our duties. The chunks of wood were dropped with improving accuracy and fell as silent as dew and as humane as a headache. Animal control was our business, the Humane Society we were not. We diligently carried out our form of animal control until we ran out of firewood.

While our animal control efforts were around 99 percent effective, Queenie demonstrated the importance of that remaining one percent by producing a litter of puppies almost every year. Two of those pups were aptly named Meathead and Jughead. Meathead found a home with a man who needed a guard dog at a logging camp, while Jughead ended up with some folks from (of all places) TOWN!

On Burn Hill, there were animals that defied control. Wild animals were one of the reasons I feared the dark. Making the long journey to the outhouse after sunset was dreaded by every child in the family. Although it was never explicitly stated, at least among the boys, it was deemed acceptable to relieve oneself almost anywhere outside.

One cold, wintry night, a trip to the outhouse was not part of my plans. I stepped out onto the front porch and stood there for a while, surveying the darkness. All was silent. The moon provided just enough light to reveal a few vague features in the front yard. I could make out the snowball bush and the lilac bush—the only two landscaping elements in the yard. Tentatively, I took a step off the porch, and even that slight sound sent a shiver down my slender back.

As I began to water the grass, I noticed a shadowy movement from behind the lilac bush. I froze midstream, my eyes straining to see, yet not wanting to see. I wanted to sprint back to the house, but for some reason, I couldn't move. For several minutes, I stood transfixed, hoping to see nothing but a lilac bush.

Then, there it was, movement once again, slow and close to the ground. I could see its eyes staring directly at me, its long body and tail discernible. It was a cougar! I watched, unable to move, as it slowly flattened itself almost completely to the ground, becoming nearly invisible. Invisible, but still very much a cougar.

At that moment, without any conscious effort on my part, my legs began to churn. How I managed to reach the porch and rush inside the front door remains a mystery, as the next moment found me standing inside the front door of the house, my overalls unbuttoned and hanging loosely around my knees.

For a couple of minutes, I couldn't speak. A shiver reverberated through my entire body. "You look like you've seen a ghost," Dave remarked.

"And you've peed all over yourself," someone else chimed in.

"What was it?" asked Mutt, making the most sensible inquiry from this group of spectators. "IT WAS A LION, IT WAS A LION," I gasped.

———— ·+· ————

Some nights on the farm were eerily still—too still. On those nights every animal's instinct compelled them to lay low. The cow in the barn, the cat on the woodpile, and the dog on the back stoop all sensed the same unknown presence. It was a night so quiet that even the owls remained silent. Nerves were taut, and every creature waited with wide-open eyes.

Then, suddenly, the wait was over, and the silence shattered into a cacophony of terrifying, horrifying sounds—chickens under attack. Each member of the Hale family found themselves trembling and wide awake, standing in the darkness of the living room. Someone fumbled to light a kerosene lamp.

"It's a cougar," someone whispered.

Dealing with this kind of animal control required men of courage and tenacity, and dogs with character and sharp teeth. Dave and Odin wasted no time equipping themselves with loaded rifles and a lantern. Once prepared, they hurried across the yard towards Dave's battered 1938 International truck. The old truck sputtered and roared to life, and even Queenie appeared energized and ready for action.

The old International truck was not made for speed, and we all hoped it would make it to the chicken house in time. With Dave flooring the pedal and the headlights piercing through the night, the old truck barreled across the yard, splashed through the creek, and rattled across the field toward the chicken house. Queenie, resembling a fierce junkyard dog, trotted alongside the roaring truck.

Killing the engine and rolling to a stop, Dave and Odin leaped out, rifles at the ready. The chicken house stood eerily quiet, but Queenie seemed hesitant to enter. Clutching his bolt-action Savage rifle, Dave cautiously approached the entrance. With the muzzle of his rifle, he gingerly pushed open the creaky door. Odin followed closely, holding the flickering kerosene lantern high, illuminating the black void beyond the threshold. The shadows within danced and swayed to the rhythm of the lantern as Dave positioned himself for action. Holding his rifle at his right hip, Dave strained his eyes, attempting to discern meaning within the shifting shadows.

"What is it?" Odin whispered.

"It's a, it's a ..."

"What is it?" Odin pleaded.

"It's ... it's gone," Dave stammered.

Inside, a few lifeless chickens lay scattered, but the rest of the flock huddled together in a corner, all scratching desperately to reach the bottom.

What had viciously attacked the chickens? Whatever it was, it had vanished. And luckily for it, it hadn't encountered two wide-eyed riflemen and a fierce junkyard dog.

Pa and Ma in 1945, with the first half of their family.
Dave, Priscilla, Odin and Marilyn

———— •+• ————

CHAPTER TWO

THE BULL

E very smart city kid knows that a calf is just a calf until it has a calf, and then it becomes a cow. But a farm kid's understanding goes deeper and is far more practical. It goes like this: a calf is a calf until it has a calf, and then it becomes a cow—unless, of course, it's a bull. This kind of knowledge gives farm kids an edge when it comes to survival.

On a relatively dull afternoon, Mutt and I found ourselves wandering aimlessly in the field. There was no specific reason for our wandering, but sometimes in our aimlessness, we would stumble upon something to do. The bull, on the other hand, had good reason to be in the field and was presently eyeing us with evil intent. This we should have recognized, because the bull was practicing take-offs and landings.

It's worth noting that a bull has only two reasons for being on a farm: one is to provide a touch of fear in an otherwise tranquil and peaceful setting. So, when you have two farm kids aimlessly wandering in a field and a bull seeking revenge, you could sell tickets to city kids. And when you have two skinny farm kids in a field with no particular purpose, and one bull searching for a target, it's the perfect scenario for one of those skinny kids to be wearing a bright red coat.

Mutt was dressed in her brown play coat, which had been passed down from our oldest sister, Priscilla. As for me, I didn't have a coat with any historical background, but my red coat was about to make its mark in my own personal history.

Little did I anticipate the fascination the bull would have with my vibrant red coat. My older brothers were quick to point out that I had the perfect coat to catch the bull's attention. They even suggested that I parade around the field wearing it.

Realizing the intense interest the bull had in my red coat, I decided to take it off and wave it around by the sleeves, ensuring the bull's attention wouldn't wane. Just as I was starting to lose interest in the coat-waving game, Mutt shouted, "Cramp!" I looked up to see the beast charging straight towards us, wild-eyed, nostrils flared, and tail erect. For a brief moment I stood there, contemplating the wonders of this powerful and dangerous creature, marveling at how much city kids were missing out on. But then, I remembered something I had learned in school, a fact that had never seemed vital until that very moment: The shortest distance between point "A" and point "B" is a straight line. And so, after a brief moment of running in place, I set off in a straight line towards the barn. To my surprise, the bull had also grasped this fundamental principle and was applying it with remarkable speed and precision. Although Mrs. Snyder, my third-grade teacher, had failed to teach me the meaning of "A" and "B," I quickly deduced that "A" stood for "Accelerate" and "B" stood for the "Barn."

Mutt and I had no aversion to running, but why did they have to build the barn so far from point A? As we raced towards the distant barn, the thought occurred to me that, being the male figure, I should lead the way to safety. But there was no chance of overtaking Mutt. Her skinny legs were a blur, and the clods of sod she churned up hindered my visibility.

As we approached the barn, I could see through the dust and clods that the narrow side door was closed. However, with incredible timing and agility, Mutt managed to leap up the three entry steps and swing open the door in one swift motion. I followed closely behind, gasping for air as we sprinted into the barn.

The bull should have realized that the door was not intended for massive beasts like itself but rather for farmers. Yet, paying little regard to design or architecture, the bull charged up the steps, squeezed through the narrow doorway, and entered the barn.

With our sanctuary rudely invaded, we sought the ultimate refuge—the haymow. Before the bull could engage us physically, we sprinted for the stairs and ascended swiftly to the safety of the haymow. Although safety pins and safety goggles are typically associated with the word "safety," the haymow could hardly be described as such. Dusty, dim, and filled with spiders, it was far from a secure haven. But in this chaotic moment, safety was a relative concept.

Before we could catch our breath and inhale the dusty air, the bull charged up the stairs after us. It became evident that elevation was our key to survival. Hastily, Mutt and I climbed the walls, scrambling to the safety of one of the rafter ties high above the haymow floor. It's curious to think that I would describe these lofty rafter ties as safe, considering that just weeks earlier, I had fallen from one and had the wind knocked out of me. It was a memorable experience, with Mutt leaning over me, her eyes filled with sympathy, a look I had never seen before nor seen since.

From our prime seats high on a stadium rafter tie, we watched with wide-eyed amazement as the bull crashed through the boards of the haymow floor. Board after board snapped like popsicle sticks under the beast's heavy weight. Massive holes now perforated the floor as the beast awkwardly slid and stumbled.

The rodeo show came to an abrupt end without an encore when the bull charged out of the large mow door and landed with a deafening thud on the ground several feet below. With our limbs trembling uncontrollably, we descended to the mow floor and approached the open door. Peering down at the scene of the fall, we were astonished to see the bull standing, seemingly unscathed, as if to say, "No problem here." It was clear that the bull was attempting to act as though nothing had happened.

"Cramp," Mutt said, her voice tinged with smugness, "city kids could never survive on a farm."

"Y-y-yeah," I stammered, my voice high-pitched with nervousness, "they'd probably be scared to death of a bull."

Low budget farming on Burn Hill in 1945. Pa, Dave and Odin load hay onto a wagon being towed with the family's 1932 Plymouth.

CHAPTER 3

————— ·+· —————

OUTBUILDINGS

Merriam-Webster's Dictionary defines an outbuilding as "a building separate from, and subordinate to, the main house." While the outbuildings on the Hale farm may have been considered subordinate, their significance should not be underestimated. These structures, despite their shabby appearance, hold significant memories.

If the measure of a farm's worth is based on its outbuildings, then Burn Hill Farm would rank among the finest. In addition to treehouses and forts, our farm boasted six main outbuildings: the pumphouse, woodshed, toolshed, barn, chicken house, and, of course, the outhouse.

The chicken house, a derelict-looking structure, was located at the western edge of the farm. While this chicken hotel faced the open field, its rear abutted the woods. Undoubtedly, this strategic positioning allowed cunning wild animals to slink from the forest to the chicken house unnoticed. A cougar or coyote could silently enter, snatch a few hens, and vanish into the woods before the farmer could even fasten his overalls.

The chicken house served as the site of my first and, as fate would have it, final parachute jump. The chosen equipment, resembling a genuine parachute except for its color, had once belonged to Walt and Ethel, a couple who worked with Pa at the box factory. Walt had bestowed upon Pa an assortment of practical and less practical items, including a rusted bicycle with two flat tires, a crank-up Victrola record player, and an oversized black umbrella. As soon as the umbrella was unfurled, everyone exclaimed, "Oh! What a huge umbrella!" Meanwhile, I quietly mused to myself, What a perfect parachute. Although perfection might not have been an accurate assessment, its destiny had been sealed.

Employing the most rudimentary principles of aerodynamics, I skillfully repurposed the umbrella into a contraption I called "Big Black." Using pilfered clothesline cord, I transformed it into a bona fide parachute. With this marvelous engineering feat complete, I proudly and discreetly transported it to the roof of the chicken house.

Of all the buildings on the farm, the chicken house had been carefully selected as the ideal launchpad. The pumphouse roof would have provided an excellent platform, but this building was too near the house, and it was important that this first jump be performed without an audience. The towering barn, while an option, sent shivers down my spine at the mere thought of standing atop it. In contrast, the chicken house roof was both far from the main house and less intimidating in terms of height. And in the unlikely event of a mechanical malfunction, I figured my chances of survival remained at a relatively favorable fifty-fifty.

With parachute in hand, I positioned myself at the highest edge of the chicken house roof, assessing the wind. To my disappointment, I found conditions favorable for the jump. I reassured myself that Big Black was a marvel of engineering and possessed all the necessary qualities for a successful descent. Yet, a certain uneasiness churned within me—a familiar sensation I assumed all skydivers experience before taking the great plunge.

Clutching the cords tightly in both hands, I leaned forward over the roof's edge. I anticipated my feet propelling me into the air, but they hesitated. The more I leaned, the firmer my toes gripped the roof's edge.

I recall the sudden yank that lifted my feet from the roof, causing the parachute to flutter wildly. The landing eludes my memory, but I do know it was not a graceful touchdown on my feet. When consciousness returned, I found myself entangled in cords, perched unceremoniously amidst a pile of soft, odorous matter that farmers refer to as "the real thing."

The pumphouse held a special place in my heart. It was a small, weathered building with a shed-type roof that extended several feet over the doorway. The roof served as an ideal spot for drying prunes, effectively extending the prune season by several weeks.

The pumphouse involved two elementary but essential elements: the well and the pump. The well was the source of water for the home, and the pump was the machinery to get it there. These two components worked together seamlessly, as long as there was water in the well.

A wise and philosophical man once shared a thought-provoking statement: "A well is something surrounding nothing, or nothing surrounded by something." This profound observation perfectly encapsulated our well. During the months of July to September, the well ran dry, leaving both the pump and the Hale household parched.

Behind the pumphouse was a concrete slab. Set neatly into this slab was a short length of two-by-four with a sixteen-penny nail protruding from it—cleverly disguised, but a lid nonetheless. When I lifted it out, I could gaze down into the bowels of the earth. What if I fell in? What if no one heard me yell? No one would know how I struggled and struggled and almost climbed out. The thoughts were pure terror, but I enjoyed them anyway.

Although the temptation to drop stones into the well was strong, we were firmly instructed not to do so, and thus refrained from it. After all, prune pits served as a suitable alternative.

It wouldn't be true country living without the presence of tree houses. In our case, the Hale Farm boasted two, and possibly three, tree houses. Allow me to elaborate.

Dave and Odin were renowned for their tree house construction skills—not because the structure they built was grandiose, but because it posed a formidable challenge to climb into. Perched high atop a sprawling alder tree in the woods, adjacent to a seasonal pond, this tree house featured walls, a roof, and a small window opening. The climb was so treacherous that only Dave and Odin possessed the courage to venture up, let alone risk their lives to erect it in the first place. I, on the other hand, made numerous attempts to scale the ladder-like two-by-fours nailed to the tree, yet my efforts to reach the portal of the tree house defied my every attempt.

My older brothers, being architectural prodigies, had constructed a tree house that only they could enjoy. Gaining access to their tree house would have been a proud achievement for me, and I made several valiant efforts to do so. On occasion, I managed to ascend high enough to touch the bottom of the tree house. However, this is where the real challenge began. To proceed further, one had to crawl out onto a four-inch-diameter branch several feet away, freeing oneself from the confines of the tree house's floor, in order to reach up and grasp a higher branch. From there, it was necessary to swing a leg up and over the upper branch to gain entry into the shack. I had watched Dave and Odin execute this daunting maneuver with ease. As they entered their teenage years, their interest in the tree house waned, and the lofty citadel sat abandoned and unvisited.

Now, at the tender age of eight, it was my turn to claim ownership of the lofty retreat in the massive tree.

"Why are your legs trembling?" Mutt called from the base of the tree, observing me perched at a height I had reached on numerous occasions, just beneath the tree house's floor.

"It's not my legs; it's the altitude," I weakly replied.

"Just crawl out onto that limb. It looks strong enough," Mutt encouraged.

Knowing what needed to be done and envisioning the necessary moves to enter the tree house were the easy parts. Coaxing my body to comply with my commands proved to be an entirely different challenge.

"The longer you cling to the tree, the worse it will get," Mutt advised, offering practical guidance but lacking inspiration.

"Do you want to give it a try?" I asked.

"Are you out of your mind?" Mutt retorted. "That looks like a good way to get killed."

Regrettably, I never had the opportunity to behold the interior of that tree house, and to this day, I reflect upon my unsuccessful attempts. But I am still alive.

Fortunately, I eventually found success in constructing another tree house of my own in the grand birch tree near the corner of the barn. I ensured its design was safer and easier to access, without inducing altitude sickness.

Obtaining the necessary materials to build the tree house proved to be a challenge. The meager scraps of lumber Pa had stored on the property were off-limits. Instead, I salvaged lumber from a collapsed chicken house on the neighboring Norman Melum farm, situated to the east of our farm. The chicken house had succumbed to the weight of a heavy snowstorm several years prior, leaving a pile of debris, so I helped myself to this ample resource of building materials.

Not only did I salvage the required lumber, but I also procured nails. There was a coffee can full of rusty used nails in the pump house, but this stash was Pa's and off -limits to me as well. It was common for people of lesser means to salvage used nails.

Constructing anything with used nails proved to be an exercise in futility. While one might succeed in straightening a bent nail, more often than not it would fold over as one attempted to drive it into the wood. I had to grapple with this frustrating reality. In my tree house project, if a nail started to bend during hammering, I simply struck it harder, mashing it sideways and flattening it against the wood. The results were far from aesthetically pleasing, but I managed to make at least one nail out of ten serve its intended purpose.

The grand birch tree, with its sprawling horizontal branches, was an ideal choice for my tree house. Devoid of an inspector's presence, I daresay the construction went rather smoothly for a young lad employing salvaged boards from Mr. Melum's collapsed chicken house and using recycled nails. My tree house ultimately took the form of a six-foot-by-six-foot platform. While my intention was to eventually construct walls and a roof for the tree house, I found contentment in what might be described as a tree deck for the time being.

My tree- house-building adventure held an additional feature that hadn't crossed the minds of Dave or Odin. A few feet away, in another section of the tree, I constructed an outhouse. This also was a mere deck without walls—essentially a potty with a territorial view.

I hope you don't think I built a bucket into the floor of my outhouse. That is what a city person might think appropriate. To build a practical tree outhouse, one must consider the unappealing aspect of cleaning the bucket. I had no intention of sitting over a bucket on the floor of my outhouse; that would be utter madness.

Instead, I found a keyhole saw in Pa's green metal toolbox. With it, I cut a somewhat circular hole with a diameter of approximately twelve inches in the floor.

For the next step in outhouse functionality, Mutt and Batis lent their assistance. "When I drop a rock, mark the spot where it lands," I instructed.

"But what if there's wind?" Batis pondered, displaying foresight that was perhaps too logical.

Adjusting for windage had not crossed my mind at that moment.

"We just need to get this done; we can worry about windage later."

Do you think the inventor of the wheel obsessed over what-ifs? Did Edison contemplate the what-if's when he touched two wires together, allowing electricity to pass through a glass bulb? I think not.

"Here goes; I'm dropping the rock."

Upon marking the spot where the rock landed, we proceeded to dig a hole approximately twelve inches in diameter and two feet deep.

Pa inquired about the hole within the fenced corral area of the barn, expressing concern that the cow could injure itself. I was promptly instructed to fill the hole.

The hole was eventually filled, but not before I made a trip to the tree outhouse for a private recreational experience. Perhaps it was an exceptionally windy day or there was an odd gravitational vortex in the vicinity, but things did not go as planned.

A mulligan refers to a second chance to perform an action. As a young country boy, I was unaware of this term. Golfers often call for a mulligan to take another shot, but the rules governing outhouse toilets did not allow for such leniency.

The wayward deposit was promptly scooped up and placed within the hole, which was then filled. The cow seemed content.

No other outbuilding was as frequented as the family outhouse. This relic from a bygone era remained open twenty-four hours a day, often leading to queues during peak times.

Annually, Ma undertook the task of spring cleaning the outhouse, aiming to improve the overall experience for all who would enter. Armed with soap and water, she diligently scrubbed the bare wooden interior, meticulously cleaning the walls, floor, and seats. Ma went a step further by selecting scenic pictures from magazines, which she then pasted on the walls for the enjoyment of both young and old. The final touch was the application of a few scoops of hot lime down each hole, ensuring the outhouse was thoroughly sanitized and ready for another year of vigorous use.

Situated approximately forty yards east of our home, at the far corner of the orchard, this unique facility appeared to have been placed there by someone with a perplexing mindset. A journey to the outhouse in the middle of the night evoked sheer terror. The mere act of navigating to the two-holer under the cover of darkness could take up to ten anxiety-ridden minutes. It wasn't due to the significant distance, but rather the presence of a phenomenon known as NIGHT. There might not be a scientific name for this condition, but I would call it Darkness Paralysis Syndrome, a condition rendering one's legs immobile in response to real and imagined sights and sounds. The unfortunate child making this daunting trip had to tiptoe cautiously beneath the looming orchard trees while shining a flashlight in every direction. The sudden thud of an apple falling from a tree within the orchard was enough to paralyze the child's legs. Once immobilized, the true terror would unfold. The flashlight's beam would dim, and the unseen horrors of the orchard would negate any need for the outhouse.

Even when safely locked inside the outhouse, I couldn't shake the uncertainty of whether some creature or wild man might be peering through a knothole. The return journey home lasted a mere five seconds, during which I always managed to outrun anything that pursued me.

It remained a mystery whether the outhouse was constructed near the prune tree or if the prune tree was planted near the outhouse. Regardless of the reasoning, the Italian prune tree stood a mere fifteen feet from the two-holer, suggesting a rational mind behind the design.

One late summer afternoon, Batis and I ventured into the orchard to indulge in some prunes. Climbing the prune tree and settling onto a comfortable limb, we proceeded to devour the perfectly ripe fruit. However, after polishing off a large quantity of prunes, Batis began complaining of abdominal distress.

"Must be the altitude," I reasoned.

"It's not the altitude!" snapped Batis.

"Oh," I replied, "maybe you should ..." But before I could finish my sentence, Batis was already making his way to the outhouse. Several minutes later, I found myself pounding on the outhouse door.

"Just a minute," came the feeble reply.

"Open up!" I yelled. "You've been in there long enough to develop cabin fever."

"Okay, but you'll have to use the low hole," Batis hollered back.

Spending an afternoon in such conditions within the outhouse quickly became tiresome. While the pictures on the walls and the information on the lime sack provided some diversion, only those devoid of one of their five senses could genuinely appreciate this activity.

"I never want to see another prune again," groaned Batis as we exited the outhouse. Holding our stomachs, we made a dash for the house. Did I say dash? Even baby Bits could have outcrawled us.

The Hale family home on Burn Hill. 1945-1958

CHAPTER 4

——— ·✦· ———

BOREDOM CURES

M utt carefully uprooted a thriving weed nestled between a couple of rutabaga plants and discarded it between the rows. It was late morning, and the promise of a hot August day hung in the air. The brown earth of the vegetable garden still retained the dampness from the overnight rain, and droplets of water adorned the lush greenery. While it could have been described as a beautiful summer day on Burn Hill, the daunting task of weeding lay ahead, casting a shadow over the otherwise idyllic scene.

Behind us, the rows we had already weeded displayed the sorry remnants of once healthy-looking weeds, now withered and lifeless under the relentless sun. In stark contrast, the plump-leaved rutabagas, their edible parts bulging grotesquely from the ground, were spared our weeding efforts. The appeal of earning a mere five cents per row began to fade as we contemplated the seemingly endless expanse of rutabagas and weeds stretching before us. Mutt yanked another weed, then straightened up, stretching her back. "Five cents a row—what do you think?"

I glanced at the palm of my hand, reminiscing about the size of a nickel and imagining how a couple of them would enhance the handful of pennies inside my makeshift metal Band-Aid box bank. "Well, it's a lot of money," I replied, attempting to remain rational. However, it was too late. Boredom, predictable and merciless, had begun to lure us away from our worthwhile and profitable endeavor. The lazy summer day seemed determined to bore us to death. After all, pulling weeds was a monotonous task, and we yearned for something more exhilarating.

"Hey, I've got an idea," Mutt interjected, her enthusiasm rekindled. "Let's go scare cars!" It was as if she had discovered a new remedy for boredom, though scaring cars had been an effective cure for quite some time.

"But aren't you thirsty?" I questioned. Mutt nodded, suggesting that before we embarked on our car-scaring mission, we should ask Ma for a root beer. Ma readily complied with our request, likely empathizing with the challenging conditions we had to endure and taking into consideration the possibility of dehydration and heatstroke. Although she didn't utter a word, her nod towards the icebox conveyed her wholehearted sympathy for our plight. If there ever was a deserving duo in need of a cold root beer, it was the two rutabaga patch weeders standing in Ma's kitchen.

We opened the icebox, perusing several bottles of homemade root beer. Selecting the perfect bottle required some consideration. After all, drinking brown root beer from a green 7-UP bottle would be unseemly and potentially detrimental to the flavor. I chose a clear bottle with bold white lettering spelling "Nesbitt's." Mutt opted for a clear Nehi bottle with red labeling. All the pop bottles used for making root beer were either given to us or found along the road. Soda pop was a luxury our family couldn't afford, but with our collection of salvaged bottles, we were able to craft our own beverages.

Sipping root beer through a straw made from the stems of mature pasture grass enhanced the experience. Finding a straw of substantial diameter required a combination of patience and crawling on our bellies through the hay field. If luck was on our side, our diligence would yield the coveted "big" straw, but more often than not, we had to settle for the "skinny" straw. Savoring homemade root beer through a skinny straw could occupy an entire day, but it was the preferred way to enjoy the beverage. It necessitated a mouth capable of producing a powerful vacuum and resulted in sunken cheeks reminiscent of an elderly gentleman inhaling his dentures.

We were halfway through our root beers when a massive log truck thundered past our farm, enroute to the mill. "Hey," I exclaimed, "we should have scared him!" Discarding our homemade straws, we quickly finished our beverages and sprinted along the gravel driveway towards the road.

Scaring cars entailed utilizing the white rail fence at the edge of the road, which offered an entertaining remedy for boredom. Balancing on the top rail, we darted back and forth with practiced agility, our bare and calloused feet deftly avoiding wood splinters and avian droppings.

Having completed our warm-up routine, we perched ourselves on the rail fence, facing the road, and waited. "Shhh!" Mutt whispered, "I think I hear one approaching." Soon, a pea-green car came into view, ascending the hill at a leisurely pace. As it drew near, our excitement grew, especially upon realizing it was what we referred to as a "Gallagher car." Allow me to explain that a Gallagher car was our term for any vehicle boasting trunk dimensions comparable to a small building. The name originated from Mrs. Gallagher, the school nurse who owned a 1949 Dodge coupe. This particular Dodge model had a front seat but lacked a back seat, with the entire space behind the front seat dedicated to the trunk. The generous proportions of the bulbous trunk perfectly mirrored Mrs. Gallagher's own ample posterior. Gallagher cars were often driven by individuals who held little regard for personal dignity, prioritizing ample room for a single passenger and a trunk capable of accommodating their worldly possessions. Naïve old ladies were frequent owners of Gallagher cars, so our anticipation mounted as one approached.

We waved enthusiastically as the old lady neared our perch. She reciprocated, waving her delicate handkerchief with a broad smile. At that moment, we feigned losing our balance, swinging our arms wildly as if struggling to avoid falling in front of her car. We eagerly anticipated the old lady's reaction. With remarkable reflexes, she stomped on the brakes, possibly with both feet, causing the engine to stall abruptly as the car nosedived to a stop. It was a sight to behold—the coupe's protuberant trunk soaring high, appearing even more colossal than before. Regaining our balance, we smiled and waved to reassure her that we hadn't fallen and were perfectly unharmed.

As she settled herself behind the steering wheel, preparing to restart the Dodge, we witnessed a sudden lapse in her automotive expertise. Completely forgetting about the clutch, she attempted to start the car while still in gear. The Gallagher car jerked and lurched, eventually nose-diving as she hastily hit the brake. Once she located the clutch and managed to restart the car, she smiled at us, her composure regained, and smoothly shifted into gear. Revving the engine in preparation for departure, she released the clutch, resulting in a backward surge down the road. Slamming on the brakes, she brought the Gallagher car to a smoking halt, its nose high in the air and the ponderous trunk bowing towards the ground.

Unable to contain ourselves any longer, Mutt and I burst into the nearby hay field, rolling around in uncontrollable fits of laughter. When we finally stood up to catch our breath, all that remained was the faint aroma of burnt rubber and a wispy cloud of blue smoke lingering above the roadway. The Gallagher car had vanished.

— •+• —

If scaring cars seemed too tame, there was always the option of scaring ourselves. If you were to embark on a hike starting in the woods behind the barn, traversing southwest across the Parsons' property and continuing south through heavy forest, you would eventually stumble upon an abandoned shack nestled deep within the woods. Being the nomadic Hale children that we were, the forest could only conceal this forsaken shack for so long. It was likely Dave and Odin who first stumbled upon it, and soon enough, Mutt, Batis, Dez, and I would explore it ourselves.

Dave and Odin, with their knowledge of the property's history, claimed that many years ago, a man named Blimkey had lived there. In the Hale household, this enigmatic place was simply referred to as "Blimkey's." Given the possibility of squatters finding refuge in such properties, we knew we had to exercise caution when venturing to this location.

"Okay," Mutt said, "I think we're getting close, so let's keep our voices down." The four of us stealthily maneuvered through the trees, brush, and ferns. The dense foliage created a dimly lit and ominous atmosphere, interrupted only by the gentle raindrops trickling through the leaves.

"I see it," Batis whispered. We crouched in a thicket of ferns, observing the Blimkey shack from a mere fifty feet away. The only movement was a steady stream of water flowing off the back corner of the weathered structure.

We could discern a small back porch, measuring no more than six feet square, cluttered with debris, and a broken wooden chair leaning against the wall next to the back door. To the right of the porch, a single window remained intact. Awkwardly bent and rusty, a stovepipe jutted out from the roof.

"There's no smoke coming from the chimney," I silently mouthed. In my mind, the absence of smoke implied no occupants. "Let's go," I signaled.

"Let's wait a little longer," Mutt whispered, always the cautious one.

In a peculiar way, huddling in the ferns provided a sense of comfort, yet the shack possessed an irresistible allure. Slowly, we emerged from our hiding spot and tiptoed closer to the structure. Crossing into a small clearing, we exposed ourselves to anyone who might be inside. There was a strong urge to retreat to the ferns, but curiosity was gradually overpowering fear.

Steering clear of any direct line of sight from the window, we silently crept towards the back porch. Suddenly, Dez halted and pointed to the ground. "What?" I asked. Dez didn't respond but continued pointing at the weeds. At his feet lay tarnished brass shell casings from a high-powered rifle. Intrigued and slightly unnerved, we pocketed the casings. This discovery added another layer of unease to our encounter with BLIMKEY'S.

Batis suggested peering through the window, but none of us possessed the courage—at least not yet—to venture close to it.

On the porch, we encountered bottles, rusted cans, a half-filled wooden apple box containing wet and moldy newspapers, and a lantern without glass, hanging from a nail on the shingled wall. Among the debris, we discovered several deformed and mushroomed bullets, obviously fired into something solid and subsequently retrieved.

Imagination ran wild with such a find. "Did someone get killed?" Dez inquired.

"Maybe," I mused.

"No," countered Mutt, "Blimkey was probably just trying to save the bullets after shooting them."

"But why save them?" I questioned. None of us had a satisfactory answer.

We collected the bullets, potentially preserving them as evidence in case a crime had been committed.

Someone motioned towards the door, weathered and peeling, disintegrating at the seams. Flakes of dark green paint had accumulated in a neat line on the porch floor as they peeled off the door. I inspected the tarnished but smooth brass doorknob. Did its condition indicate someone had been frequenting this shack, or possibly living here?

Mutt gestured for us to stay away from the door. "We can't go inside until we've peeked through the window to make sure no one is in there."

Although we had postponed this act until now, we knew it had to be done.

"You do it," Mutt said, pointing at me. I wasn't thrilled with the suggestion and offered an alternative plan.

"Let's crouch below the window together and gradually raise our heads, just enough to peek in. If there's someone inside, they probably won't see us."

That became our plan, which we executed flawlessly. Simultaneously, we raised our heads until our eyes were barely above the windowsill. It took a few seconds for our eyes to adjust to the semidarkness inside the shack.

Suddenly, one of us let out a shriek, though I couldn't tell who. In a panic, we scrambled to our feet, racing away from the window. Finding shelter amidst the trees, we paused to analyze what we had witnessed.

Concealed behind a dense cluster of brush, we stared back at the window for several minutes.

The shack remained motionless and silent.

"It was a man!" we exclaimed in unison.

Each of us recounted what we had seen—a man seated rigidly upright in a chair, staring straight ahead.

"He looked ... he was ... I know he was ... he was dead," Mutt stammered.

With that description verbalized and unanimously affirmed, we sprinted through the woods, heading back home.

Sleep eluded us that night. I don't know how Mutt endured the night, but in an upstairs bedroom, three eyewitness brothers engaged in a lengthy conversation about the Burn Hill adventure that would forever be etched in our collective memories: BLIMKEY'S!

There is perhaps no event in the history of the Hale family more traumatic than the day the house caught fire. It was a day that would leave a lasting impact on everyone, except for one family member named Odin.

The summer morning started like any other, with Ma going about her usual routine of preparing breakfast. Pa had already left for work at the box factory, and Dave had also departed for his job as a whistle punk and choker setter for the Bill Roll Logging Company. Most kids at age seventeen would not be holding down a man's job, but Dave had quit school after grade eight to help with the financial burden of the family.

For the family members still at home, there was little reason to rush out of bed. Pa might have insisted on an early start, but Ma allowed the kids to sleep a little longer, likely so she could enjoy a moment of tranquility with her cup of coffee.

As the fire crackled gently in the living room heater and a pot of oatmeal simmered on the kitchen stove, the house remained still. Lazy days have a way of changing course in an instant, and on this particular day, it happened with a muffled explosion followed by a furious roar. Ma rushed outside and glanced up at the brick chimney protruding from the shingled roof of the house. To her horror, she saw a ferocious fire shooting out of the chimney.

Unbeknownst to Ma, the fire was also bursting through cracks in the mortar of the old chimney within the attic. She hurried back inside to wake the family, who were still sound asleep in the house. With Pa and Dave away at work, it was now up to Odin to take charge as the man of the house.

"Odin, the house is on fire!" Ma yelled upstairs.

Odin, his usual composed self, replied, "Call the fire department. They'll put it out."

"No, I really mean it. Get up and help! The house is on fire!" Ma's urgency grew, but Odin's response remained unchanged.

Ma's urgent call to the upstairs may not have gotten much of a stir from Odin, but the rest of the kids were immediately at Ma's side and hastily whisked out of the house. Ma continued yelling at Odin from outside, her tone shifting from urgent to angry.

"You come down here right now! You've got to ..."

Just then, Odin walked out the front door and looked up at the roof of the house. "It really is burning, ain't it?" he said, without a hint of alarm.

The roof was engulfed in flames! The cedar shingles surrounding the chimney crackled and popped under the intense heat. There was nothing to do but watch.

Ma had already called the fire department in the nearby town of Arlington, but it would take at least half an hour for the firemen to assemble and for the firetruck to navigate the slow, uphill climb over the three-mile distance.

It felt like an agonizingly long wait, but eventually, the sound of help could be heard making its way up Burn Hill. First came the wailing siren, followed by the strained rumble of a grossly underpowered truck. With the nearest fire hydrant three miles away, the only water available to fight the fire was what the old truck carried.

If you don't believe in miracles, you should.

The firefighters worked swiftly, first aiming water up at the roof from the ground and then, using a ladder, ascending to the roof to extinguish the flames. They couldn't help but marvel at how little damage the fire had caused. The fire had been burning in the attic and on the dry cedar roof for at least forty-five minutes. By all accounts, the house should have been completely destroyed.

The firefighters could only shake their heads in disbelief. Why hadn't the fire consumed the house?

YOU TELL ME.

———— ·✦· ————

On a drizzly winter evening, boredom seemed to permeate the atmosphere of the Hale household. Dave sat where one might expect to see a pan of bread dough rising—on top of the living room wood stove. This act of hot stove sitting fascinated the younger members of the family but greatly annoyed Pa. To Dave, it was an impressive trick, but Pa saw it as a disrespectful and smart-alecky behavior. However, Dave often got away with such antics, perhaps due to being the firstborn and enjoying some birthright privileges.

As Dave warmed his buns and flipped through a Popular Mechanics magazine, the dim flicker of a kerosene lamp on the pump organ provided just enough light to read the pages. The magazine was filled with incredible articles: a car with wings that actually flew, a carburetor promising one hundred miles per gallon, and a DIY porch swing you could build yourself for less than two dollars.

Suddenly there it was, on page twenty-six. The words leaped off the page—and they hurt: "Hey skinny," a big bully was saying to a wimpy-looking guy. It was an advertisement for a Charles Atlas course, promising bulging muscles for any ninety-eight-pound weakling who would invest in his course.

Dave compared the arms of the wimpy guy in the magazine to his own, particularly the area where biceps were supposed to be. He felt pity for the wimpy guy in the magazine, but mostly he felt pity for himself.

Later that evening, Dave strategically left the opened magazine on Odin's bed, turned to page twenty-six. The next day, filled with determination, Dave and Odin sent a letter and hard-earned money to Charles Atlas, marking the beginning of their journey towards acquiring bulging muscles and overcoming the boredom of long winter evenings.

The mailman grinned knowingly as he handed the package labeled "Charles Atlas" to Dave and Odin. The mailman looked like he wanted to say something but didn't. The two would-be muscle men quickly hustled the package upstairs to their bedroom. What they didn't need right now was Annie Oakley or somebody else making snide comments. Besides, the rest of the family would know soon enough when shirt seams began busting and buttons started popping. It was almost too fantastic to think about, and Dave and Odin could hardly wait.

However, the Charles Atlas package contained no bulging muscles, only diagrams and detailed instructions on how to achieve them. Disappointed but still determined, Dave and Odin began the rigorous and painful process of "bodybuilding" as outlined by Charles Atlas. Despite their efforts, no noticeable progress seemed to appear in their biceps or any other areas. Nonetheless, they remained undeterred, with Dave reassuring Odin that "these things take time."

After weeks of faithfully following the instructions, Dave and Odin examined their arms once more, focusing on the bicep area. Odin broke the silence, offering his theory: "I think I know the problem."

"Yea, so what do ya mean by that?" barked Dave.

"Well," continued Odin, "we only weigh about eighty-five pounds."

Dave stared at the floor. It was hard to accept, but ... "Let me see that magazine again," he growled. Sitting on the edge of the bed, Dave and Odin reexamined the advertisement in the magazine. Sure enough, it did specify "ninety-eight pounds," and at eighty-five pounds they simply didn't meet the requirement.

Defeated and deflated, Dave and Odin stared blankly at the pages of the magazine as Odin flipped them in despair. Suddenly, there it was, on page fifty-seven; the words seemed to jump right off the page. "Earn this Genuine Western Acoustical Guitar by selling only 150 packets of flower and vegetable seeds."

The next day Odin put a letter to the seed company in the mailbox and flipped up the little red flag. Running back to the house, Odin thought about the timing of this endeavor. With spring just around the corner, many people would be anxious to buy seeds from him, and he could earn the "Genuine Western Acoustical Guitar."

Every day Odin sprinted out to the road to check the mailbox to see if the sales kit and seeds had arrived. Most days the box contained only the usual: a bill or an occasional letter, and sometimes what we called "fan mail." Fan mail was always fun and interesting and is the same kind of mail that people now call "junk mail."

The honk, honk, honk out at the road meant only one thing, and Odin reacted accordingly. The mailman had indeed done the honking and had left a brown package tied with string hanging from the latch hook on the mailbox door. Odin lifted the package from off the hook and read the label, which confirmed it contained the long-awaited sales kit and seeds. Odin turned and began to slowly walk back to the house. Whirling in his mind was a fantasy exciting and wonderful, and the package he clutched in his hands would make the dream a reality. The walk to the house became a dreamy walk to stardom as his thoughts played with a future scene ...

A hush falls on the gathering crowd of neighbors and passers-by as he steps forward on the front porch. The beautiful guitar is slung casually from his shoulder, reflecting the headlights of cars arriving in the yard. The gathering audience is riveted in attention as his fingers strike a single vibrant chord. And then as he strikes another chord, his own deep mellow voice combines in resonating harmony ...

"Whatcha got there, Dreamer?" queried Annie Oakley. "I said, whatcha got there?"

"Huh? Oh. Ah, a guitar, I mean seeds," mumbled Odin, as the real world tumbled back into place.

Odin wouldn't let this one momentary lapse from reality sidetrack him from the task that lay ahead. On the other hand, I don't think Annie Oakley was overly impressed with Odin's career as a seed salesman. Annie, despite her unglamorous nickname, considered herself destined for a life of status and grandeur. She sometimes would tell us younger kids that she had "royal blood." Whatever that meant.

Ma bought a few packets of seeds, and so did a couple of people at the Acme box factory where Pa worked, but Odin mostly concentrated his selling efforts on the Burn Hill folk. The sales kit contained the dos and don'ts of salesmanship, things like how to dress, what to say and, of course, what not to say. An example of what not to say would be as follows: "Hello, Mr. Neighbor, my name is Odin Hale. You wouldn't want to buy some seeds, would you? Oh, I didn't think you would since you never grow a garden anyway. Well, thanks just the same. See ya."

Just what Odin's particular sales pitch sounded like, I cannot say, as none of us ever heard it. Although in his sleep one night he was heard to mutter, "Nup nup seed seed." A linguistic specialist might be required to interpret these utterings, but I'm thinking the interpretation might be "Buy the seeds, you cheapskate," or possibly it could mean "Help make me a guitar legend." Whatever magic words were spoken into the ears of Burn Hill folk is unknown, but one thing was certain: Seeds were selling and selling well.

The diminishing burden of seed packets only intensified his yearning for the guitar, as each day he planned his sales route. After pumping and coasting his bicycle up and down Burn Hill and giving his sales pitch to all the farmers, semi-farmers, and wannabe-farmers, Odin had sold all but a few packets of seeds. Odin sold to the Sancrant family down the hill and to Mrs. Parsons down by the pond. Up the hill he sold to Mrs. Sundquist and to Gus and Helga Zaretzke. Mr. Robison actually purchased the most packets. His wife Lena would plant them, of course, and grow them, and harvest them, and cook them, and Mr. Robison would eat them, of course. Such was the non-stellar reputation of Mr. Robison.

Ma bought up the few remaining seed packets, including enough rutabaga seeds to ensure a bumper crop of the dreaded veggie, while Pa seemed pleased with a packet labeled "Ground Cherries" and was anxious to try them.

Finally, one day the mailman again honked as he drove into the yard. He parked his old sedan next to the snowball bush and shut the engine off. All the Hales spilled out of the house and onto the front porch to see what would inspire such a personal visit from the US Postal Service. While mail delivery was daily except Sundays, it was most unusual for mail to be brought right to our front door.

We could see the mailman through the dirty windshield, sitting where one might expect a rural postal driver to be sitting, almost entirely on the right, in the passenger seat. This was the style of our Burn Hill mailman and probably every other rural postal driver in the country. To a city dweller it may seem strange to learn that rural postal drivers often used their own personal cars to deliver mail and preferred to sit on the right side of the car, even though the steering wheel and all the other important mechanical controls were on the other side of the car. Of course, there was a very sensible reason for this phenomenon, which all country folk understand. I did wonder if, after completing his route, our mailman slid over and sat behind the steering wheel, or did he motor on home still near the right side of the car?

The mailman emerged from the car with a large package wrapped in brown paper. Upon seeing the package, Odin jumped off the porch and confidently accepted the package. "It's my guitar," he proudly proclaimed. When he returned to the porch, he immediately proceeded to tear open the package, with not a single glance at his admiring family.

Slowly Odin lifted something green out of the box. It was a guitar, all right. It was bigger than a ukulele, but not by much. Odin looked at the guitar and then at us. Nobody smiled and nobody laughed. It was as if we'd all been duped, we had all been cheated. The undersized green guitar was made of pressed pulpboard and had pictures of cowboys painted on it. Odin slammed the guitar back into the box, and with package in hand he ran through the house and out the back door. I never saw that cardboard guitar again, and I never asked about it.

That night after Odin and Dave had retired to their bedroom, Odin spotted the Popular Mechanics magazine lying on the floor. Picking it up, he examined page fifty-seven and scoffed at the picture of the "Genuine Acoustical Guitar." He walked slowly to the open window and stared blankly into the spring night. Angrily he twisted the magazine into a tight roll and repeatedly smacked it against the window frame. Just before he could hurl it into the blackness, Dave shouted, "Hey, don't throw that out the window! I saw a deal in there about making over a hundred dollars a month just by addressing envelopes for some company and sending them to people."

Odin pulled back the blankets of his bed, propped his pillow up against the wall and crawled in. As he did so, he asked, "What page is it on?"

Summer of 1953. Andrew and Marilyn with the two youngest, Sharon, and Stephen. Queenie was always happy to be included in a photo. The few chickens in the background seem unaware that history was being recorded.

CHAPTER 5

—•◆•—

THE RIFLEMAN

T he door swung open, and I stepped out into the bright sunlight. I nudged the door shut with my foot, standing with my feet wide apart, my finger nervously fondling the trigger. I squinted in the bright sunlight and tugged at the brim of my hat to shade my eyes. All was still, the kind of stillness that made a man uneasy. The rifle was kept level at my hip and ready.

Slowly, I surveyed my surroundings. A banty hen, unaware of my presence, busily dusted herself in the powdery loam below the kitchen window. Tar Baby, the cat, lay sprawled out in the dirt near the woodshed. A dog that looked vaguely familiar lay motionless not more than ten paces from where I stood. The dog lazily opened one eye and gave me a quick glance. The dog never moved, a sure sign that it was about to attack ...

I took a few cautious steps toward the animal, all the while keeping my rifle level and steady. Still, the dog did not move. The closed eyes I took as a sure sign that the dangerous beast was contemplating a sudden attack. I took another very careful step, and now I was only three paces from the beast.

I should have feared the ferocious canine, but I was packing a rifle of deadly power. I did not fear in the slightest. I continued to stand my ground, waiting for the beast to respond. One eye opened and took a quick glance in my direction.

"Whatcha lookin' at, dog?" I growled.

The dog closed its eye. I would not be fooled by that trick.

"You can close your eye, but I'm still here lookin' at ya." The dog we called Queenie didn't move.

"All right, put your paws in the air. Ya make one false move and I'll plug ya." A tail twitched. An eyebrow lifted slightly, but the eye remained closed.

"Think I'm bluffin', do ya?"

The tail began to brush back and forth on the bare dirt, like a whisk broom creating a small dust storm.

"Dust is risin' there, pooch; ya see it? That means a rain squall is a-brewin.'"

Queenie got up and licked the muzzle of my rifle. No matter how dangerous I must have appeared, the dog seemed unimpressed. Licking the business end of a rifle is a dangerous thing to do, but Queenie did not appear to have even the slightest smidgeon of fear.

The weapon in my hand was a Remington Model 510, a single-shot .22 caliber bolt-action rifle. It had been a gift to Dave and Odin from Grandpa Hale. If Dave or Odin knew that I was messing around with their gun, I'd be in a heap of trouble. But they didn't know, and they wouldn't know—they were not home. I knew that somewhere in the house there was a box or two of .22 shells, but they had been well hidden for obvious reasons.

Gun safety was a big issue with Pa, and he drilled it into each of us. Pa did not like toy guns around the house. He often said, "Guns are for killing, not for playing." I had shot the .22 on a few privileged occasions, but only under the careful supervision of Pa.

Today, while most of the family was away, I would relax the rules of gun safety. Although the gun was not loaded, it still looked mighty dangerous, and I would see to it that danger and fear would rule the day.

Queenie looked like she wanted to say something but just stood there looking up at me. She was not in the mood for acting scared, not even with the Burn Hill Rifleman leveling a gun at her.

"Okay," I said, "you can tag along, but keep an eye out for trouble, 'cause trouble is a-brewin'."

I didn't have to look far for trouble. There were two goats behind the woodshed, feeding on the weeds and brush that grew along the creek. The two goats were smart and cocky critters, despite their unglamorous names, Smelly Beck and Betty Grey Butt. These two would likely try to get the jump on me, so stealth would be required. I kept my back against the side of the woodshed and moved cautiously to the corner, peeking around. Smelly Beck was staring right at me. I blamed our discovery on Queenie and gave her a stern fall-back hand signal. We retreated to conceal our presence and to consult about our next move. We would wait a few minutes and then attack around the opposite side of the woodshed. Queenie was quite willing to fall back and took the opportunity to lay down. I motioned her back up.

The attack would be decisive, swift, and unexpected. I ordered Queenie to stay two paces behind. We hid ourselves around the corner of the woodshed until I could hear the critters chomping on the brush. The goats were only a dozen quick strides away. I glanced at Queenie and gave the nod. We charged the two unsuspecting goats.

What happened next was indeed decisive, swift, and unexpected. At about the midpoint of my charge, Smelly Beck and Betty Grey Butt shot straight up into the air, and when they came down, they had already adjusted their bodies to be in full-flight attack mode in my direction. It is correct to say MY direction because Queenie was still hiding around the corner of the woodshed. I was on my own.

Smelly and Betty were a leaping, dancing pair of eight legs and four sharp horns. Their arrival was swift and purposeful. Betty snagged the rifle and sent it flying, while Smelly hit me square in the chest. I hit the ground with a thud. Smelly had knocked the wind out of me. I managed to gasp something similar to speech that sounded like "Smeeeeeell-heeee, it's meeeeeee-heeeee."

The goats did not charge again but looked at me as if to say, "That was fun, can we do it again?" Queenie had now arrived on the scene of the battle and was assessing the carnage like a war correspondent taking notes to send to the press. I lay groaning and trying to force some air into or out of my lungs. Queenie licked my face. Dogs don't seem to realize that this form of sympathy is unwelcome and downright disgusting. Just in the nick of time, and before I expired, my desperate attempts to breathe were rewarded. Air is such a wonderful thing! I lay for a while, thinking about the wonders of air and life.

The Rifleman staggered to his feet, while Smelly Beck and Betty Grey Butt prepared for another round. I moved slowly to pick up the rifle, not wanting to give any impression that I was hankering for more excitement. The rifle was undamaged; for that, I was relieved. I cleaned a little dirt off the barrel and flicked two clay-like marbles from the stock. "Disgusting," I said. Queenie seemed to agree.

It took a few more minutes for the swagger to return, but return it did.

"What did ya think of that gun battle?" I asked Queenie, but she had thought better of being my sidekick and was gone. She probably wouldn't have been overly impressed with my swagger at that moment, having just witnessed two friendly goats kick the snot out of me.

I would travel alone. A man can live without a dog, but he cannot get far in life without a gun.

The Remington .22 was not the first weapon I had mastered. Long before I was a rifleman, I had cut my teeth on a couple of other weapons: the slingshot and a BB gun. Come to think of it, my first score on a target had come in Mrs. Frazer's fourth-grade class. We were all quietly taking a written test. Mrs. Frazer was slowly strolling through the rows of desks to ensure that no one was cheating. As she passed my desk, I reached into the storage space under the desktop and pulled out a fat rubber band. I snapped it off, hitting her square on her ample backside. She felt nothing through her heavy wool dress, and she only knew that something sinister had taken place by the outburst of laughter from the class. She reversed course and stopped to pick up the rubber band that lay on the floor. The laughter abruptly stopped. Without saying a word, she held it up for all to see. She then did a thirty-second slow rotation, glaring into the eyes of the innocent students. After a long period of awkward silence, she spoke, the authority in her voice reverberating off the walls.

"You may resume your work."

She stood for another lengthy stretch of time and then spoke again.

"And whoever did this is to see me at recess."

Right, I thought. Like someone would actually volunteer to miss recess for no other purpose than to confess a shooting. When the recess bell sounded, all the kids were quick to their feet, but not as quick as Mrs. Frazer. She stood in the doorway, blocking any attempt to escape.

"Must the entire class miss recess just because no one will confess?"

Immediately, there were a dozen fingers pointing at me. That day I learned one of the fundamentals of human social behavior: Loyalty will only hold up until recess is about to be denied.

The classroom was empty in a flash.

Mrs. Frazer handed me an eraser and said, "It didn't hurt, but I insist on respect." Then she added, "Blackboard duty for a week."

When the recess gang returned, I was allowed to go back to my desk. Looking around, I could sense that I was being hailed a hero. Some kids went out of their way to walk past my desk. Some tapped gently on my desk as they passed, and others gave me a quick nod of approval. A couple of girls even smiled and winked. At that moment, I learned yet another aspect of human social behavior: A small act of civil disobedience can turn one into a classroom hero.

Moving on from the simplicity of a fat rubber band, the next step in the progression of weaponry for many is the slingshot. Mine was a homemade creation, much like many of the tools and implements on the Burn Hill farm.

The best slingshots were crafted from forked branches of vine maple and finding the perfect one was a challenge in itself. After cutting a forked branch from the tree, the bark was stripped, and the slippery sap scrubbed off. All that was needed then was a tongue cut from an old leather shoe and two long, skinny strips of rubber cut from a bicycle inner tube. Once assembled, it was best to practice firing rocks at something large to hone your accuracy. I started by aiming at the side of the barn, and with practice, I became capable of hitting a moving cow from fifty feet away.

The rhythmic hum of an aircraft interrupted my slingshot practice, drawing me away from the barn. A small, light blue plane with a white tail flew directly overhead, causing Batis and Dez to run out into the field, yelling and waving their arms. It was our customary behavior whenever an airplane violated our sovereign airspace. Usually, our antics went unnoticed, but occasionally we were rewarded with a traditional wing dip from the pilot.

This time, however, the small blue plane with the white tail did not dip its wing. Instead, it made a tight turn and flew back over us. Once again, we hooted, hollered, and ran around, waving our arms as if performing an aboriginal war dance. Little did we know, the pilot had more in store for us.

The plane returned yet again, this time flying low and fast straight at us. We screamed a mixture of delight and fear. What was this crazy pilot trying to prove? We watched as the plane climbed, regained altitude, and then made another turn toward us. It was diving hard and fast, and we quickly realized that the middle of the field was not the safest place to be. We began running toward the barn, but the roar of the plane closing in behind us made us stop and turn to face the enemy, just like facing an attacking Japanese Zero at Pearl Harbor. There was nowhere to hide.

Instincts for survival kicked in, and I reached into my back pocket for the slingshot. I wasn't thinking so much about destroying the enemy aircraft as I was desperate to do something. In my front pocket, I had a couple of stones, one of which I quickly loaded into the slingshot. The plane, which had seemed small before, was now fast approaching. I pulled back and fired, and there was the distinct sound of something striking metal.

"You hit it! You hit it!" Batis and Dez yelled. "You hit that plane. You hit it good!" We stood there in shock, disbelief, and fear. There was no mistaking it—I had shot an airplane. The sound of the stone hitting the aircraft was as clear as if I had fired a rock at a milk can. We stood amazed and dumbfounded, staring into the sky. The airplane disappeared over the tree line behind the barn and did not return. We listened until the steady hum faded into the distance.

That night at supper, the incident became a lively topic of discussion. Most at the table didn't believe the story. How could a plane fly low enough to be hit by a stone from a slingshot? How could you hit something flying that fast? Despite the doubters and scoffers, there were three determined witnesses who refused to back down. We were questioned about how we knew the rock hit the plane and what it sounded like. Batis described it as a "ponk" sound, while Dez said it sounded more like a "thunk." I simply stated that it sounded like a rock hitting an airplane.

Ma didn't say much but watched the debate unfold. Pa, on the other hand, was eager to hear all about the plane: its color, size, number of windows, wheels, and whether it was a military aircraft.

He even asked if we could see the pilot. While there were minor disagreements among the three witnesses regarding some of these details, our testimonies remained united and emphatic.

"We saw it, it tried to get us, and Cramp shot it," we affirmed.

Dave, ever the detail-oriented one, asked if we noticed what kind of motor the plane had—opposed cylinders or radial. I was glad he asked, as I could now provide a detailed description.

"It was the black kind, stuck out a little, and had a propeller on it," I explained.

Dave seemed satisfied with my response and didn't have any follow-up questions. Mutt mostly observed the lively debate but did wonder if the plane might have been damaged and crashed. I hadn't considered that possibility. Bits, busy pushing food off her highchair tray, didn't join the conversation.

Odin, with a hint of sarcasm and hearty laughter, chimed in with his parting shot: "I've heard of anti-aircraft fire from big guns, but what is this—anti-aircraft sling shooting?" He continued to mockingly laugh all the way up the stairs to his room.

Anne Oakley, appearing annoyed by the entire subject, got up and began clearing the table. While she had initially been skeptical of the airplane shooting, her parting remark offered some encouragement.

"Well, anyway, you shouldn't have been shooting at airplanes."

Although my slingshot escapades certainly earned the unvarnished admiration of my most devoted siblings, I am still of the opinion that every boy should experience the ultimate joy of receiving a BB gun for Christmas. Coloring books, Chinese checkers, and even Lincoln Logs may be forgotten, but the memory of receiving a BB gun lasts a lifetime. There is one BB gun that serves as the standard by which all others are measured: the Daisy Red Ryder. Boys start anticipating the Red Ryder under the tree around the age of six. Most fathers are ready for this momentous occasion long before mothers. Fathers believe the BB gun is age-appropriate when their sons start first grade, while mothers prefer to delay it until voting age or beyond.

From the age of six, boys eagerly anticipate this ultimate gift. They examine all the wrapped presents under the tree, searching for the one that measures exactly three inches by six inches by thirty-six inches. That's why a tape measure makes its way onto a boy's gift list starting at age five. If we consider that the purpose of wrapping a gift is to conceal its identity, then wrapping a box containing a Red Ryder is a complete waste of time and paper. Savvy little boys know the exact dimensions of a Red Ryder box, so parents often go out of their way to disguise its size. In this act of subtle selfishness, they unwittingly dampen the boy's joyful anticipation. There's nothing quite like the torturous joy of knowing what's in the box but having to wait until Christmas. Some parents even take the game to the extreme, hiding the Red Ryder in a closet and only presenting it after the coloring books, Chinese checkers, and Lincoln Logs have been opened. At that point, parents derive a twisted sense of demented satisfaction.

My Red Ryder BB gun arrived under the tree on Christmas Eve of 1955, when I was nine years old. This may have been considered a bit late, but after the airplane incident, my parents were understandably hesitant. As soon as I took the gun out of the box, Pa took it from my hands and began lecturing me about safety.

"This is not a toy," Pa emphasized, shaking the gun. Just the sound of the BBs rattling inside the gun made my heart race.

"This is a dangerous weapon," he continued, holding up a single copper-colored BB.

"You see this little BB? It comes out of the gun at 280 feet per second. That's 190 miles an hour." Even Dave and Odin paid attention.

Pa handed the gun back to me. I looked around the room, hoping everyone had noticed the significance of Pa's words. I had graduated from toys and received a dangerous weapon. I was becoming a man. Sometimes important milestones are achieved without others taking notice, but on this Christmas Eve in 1955, my entire family bore witness to this rite of passage.

Ma looked somewhat proud, even though I knew the BB gun hadn't been her idea. Dave inspected the gun but handed it back to me without comment. Odin, never one to miss an opportunity for commentary, ran his hand over my smooth cheeks and said, "That's a lot of gun for a man without even a trace of peach fuzz on his smooth little face."

I didn't expect Dave and Odin to show great enthusiasm for the gun, and they didn't. After all, they jointly owned a .22 caliber Remington rifle and had recently acquired high-power rifles. Dave had purchased a bolt-action Savage 30-30, while Odin had a lever-action Marlin 30-30. They were already seasoned veterans of a deer hunt with Pa. Although they returned from their Lake Chelan hunting trip empty-handed, that one defining experience set them apart. I couldn't argue with their achievement. They had turned peach fuzz into honest, shaveable whiskers and had gone on a rugged hunting trip. Now it was my turn to await the onset of puberty and embark on my own adventure into manhood. The Red Ryder BB gun would be just the beginning of this hazardous journey.

We always stayed up late on Christmas Eve, and Pa took the opportunity to continue drilling me about gun safety.

"Don't cock it until you're ready to fire," he warned.

This rule seemed logical, but by the time I went upstairs to bed, it was the only thing I hadn't done with the gun. I had emptied all the BBs out of the magazine and reloaded them several times. I wanted to take it outside and shoot it, but Pa said, "You must always be sure of your target, and shooting at night would not be wise."

That night before bed, I allowed my two younger brothers to admire my rifle. The three of us sat on the edge of my bed, talking about guns, shooting, and hunting. Then, I had a brilliant idea.

"Do you want to see how to cock a BB gun?" I asked.

Batis and Dez were on board, so I proceeded. Pa didn't need to know about this slight deviation from his rule. I would cock the gun that night but wouldn't fire it until morning.

I had observed others cocking their BB guns and proceeded like a pro. I set the butt end of the stock on the floor against the inside edge of my left foot, holding the rifle in my right hand. With my left hand, I pulled up on the lever. It took a mighty pull, but the rifle finally cocked. It was ready to fire. The gun now had a more menacing presence. Batis and Dez kept their distance, and I handled it with cautious reverence.

I took the rifle into bed with me that night, keeping it close at my side and tucked underneath the blankets. I moved my feet away from the muzzle, just to put my mind at ease. I played with the trigger, thinking about the day to follow when I would shoot the gun for the first time. The trigger required a considerable amount of finger pressure to fire the gun, but I wondered just how much pressure. I applied a slight squeeze, but there was no movement. I tried again, intending to apply just enough pressure to feel the trigger begin to move, then stop. Could the trigger really be that hard to budge? I squeezed a little more, and this time there was some movement.

I couldn't sleep. The trigger fascinated me, and I couldn't resist its allure. The trigger pull felt much harder than I had anticipated. I wondered if the Daisy gun company had intentionally made it difficult to safeguard small children. Then the worst thought crossed my mind—that the gun might be defective.

There was a muffled "poooof." The gun jumped in my hand, startling me, but I felt no pain in my lower extremities. I remained still.

"What was that?" Dez sat up in bed.

"It wasn't me," Batis replied.

"Well, who made that 'poooof'? That was a big one!"

"I did it," I confessed.

Someone said, "Yuck," and nothing more was said.

I fell asleep dreaming of shooting things. The small hole in my bed sheet would be discovered in the morning. It wasn't a glorious start to my shooting career, but at least I could say that my first shot wasn't a miss.

The BB gun turned out to be a very safe weapon, in the sense that I rarely hit anything with it. Birds safely flew away after the BB hit a leaf three feet away. Firing at a frog only resulted in it jumping unharmed into the creek and disappearing. Snakes presented the ultimate challenge. They always moved in the opposite direction of the gun—zigging when the gun zagged and zagging when the gun zigged.

Mice inhabited our house, though they were seldom seen. Their presence was often detected through the scratching sounds coming from within the walls. This annoyance was particularly noticeable when the house grew quiet. During the daytime, the mice refrained from any activities, as the house was usually filled with laughter, banter, and debates.

"Do you hear that scratching?" Batis asked.

We had only been in bed for a few minutes, but the house had quieted enough for the mice to take over for the night.

"Yup, I hear them," I said. "Shall we get them?"

Batis sat up in bed and shone a flashlight toward the scratching sound, coming from the corner near the ceiling. We crept out of bed to get a closer look. The scratching stopped. We waited. I had the BB gun cocked and ready. The scratching resumed, and we could see the wallpaper moving as if being chewed from the other side. This wasn't surprising, given that the wallpaper had been applied over ship-lap boards full of gaps and knot holes. It was in one of these gaps that the wallpaper was moving. Batis held the flashlight steady on the spot.

I shot from two feet away, but the BB missed the mark.

"You missed by a mile," Dez snorted.

"At least I scared them," I replied.

The scratching ceased, so we returned to bed.

But then the scratching resumed.

Batis quickly aimed the flashlight back at the spot.

"I won't miss this time," I declared. The .22 caliber rifle was just outside my door, propped up in the corner of the landing at the top of the stairs. I had a few .22 shells hidden in my sock drawer.

"Loaded and ready," I mouthed.

Learning from my previous mistake, I held the muzzle of the .22 just two inches from the vigorously wiggling wallpaper.

BOOM!

Then all was quiet, except for Ma soon appearing at the bottom of the stairs.

"What are you doing up there?"

"We shot a mouse in the wall."

Ma's response was calm and reasonable. "Well, okay, but don't damage anything."

Then the house fell silent and still.

The Rifleman slept.

A gift for my birthday. There's no joy like your first bicycle. This slick ride began as a rusty contraption with two flat tires, until Dave and Odin rebuilt it, including fresh tires and paint.

CHAPTER 6

———— •✦• ————

HAND-ME-DOWNS

The supper table was a place where many important topics were discussed and decisions were made that directly or indirectly affected my personal well-being. It was essential to not only keep track of who was reaching for seconds and who had to settle for less, but also to pay attention to the conversations around the table.

One Saturday evening, just after Pa had prayed and given God thanks for the food, and before anyone could dig into the bowl of scalloped potatoes, Ma informed Pa that I was in desperate need of new meeting clothes. I wasn't aware that my need had reached the "desperate" stage, but I assumed she was referring to my Sunday pants. "He's been growing like a weed," Ma continued. At this revelation, everyone at the table turned and stared at me in utter amazement. My sudden growth spurt had gone completely unnoticed, and now all they could do was gawk at me.

"His meeting pants are in a sorry state," Ma added, building a case for me. In moments like these, it's best to be a perfect gentleman, so I offered no advice or suggestions. Instead, I chose to sit quietly, looking needy and deserving. In an effort to demonstrate my worthiness, I assisted my little sister, Bits, by buttering her toast and helped Ma clean up the milk that Dez spilled on the floor. When I returned to the table after disposing of the milk-soaked rag, I noticed Mutt looking like she was about to be sick. A quick glance around confirmed that my thoughtful and gracious actions were making some family members a little ill.

"Well, anyway," Ma persisted, "he'll need new pants soon." Truth be told, there was nothing wrong with my meeting pants. There were no tears, holes, or stains on the fabric. I was certain that the issue wasn't the condition of the pants but rather their length. Ma could overlook the fact that my pants were a little big in the waist, as this could be fixed with a cinched belt or suspenders. However, the ten-inch gap between the cuffs and my brown oxford shoes was, in her opinion, unacceptable, even though I could compensate by pulling up my socks.

As I pondered Ma's remarks to Pa, I knew better than to get excited about the prospect of new clothes. I was well aware that "new" didn't necessarily mean brand new; in the realm of meeting clothes, "new" often meant hand-me-downs. The deceptive nature of the English language never failed to disappoint. My "new" suit would likely be an old suit handed down from either Dave or Odin. Such were the realities of my not-so-perfect world. The thought of standing in a crowd after Sunday morning meeting, dressed in a hand-me-down suit, while people made comments like, "Look at the little man today in his new suit" or "You look just like your big brother in your new suit" was an unpleasant prospect. The mere idea made me feel ill.

Pa seemed agreeable to the idea of a new suit, but he never mentioned Sears and Roebuck, Montgomery Ward, J.C. Penney, or any other clothing store for that matter. Having a full understanding of the dual definition of "new," I wasn't optimistic. What happened after supper only confirmed my suspicions that my "new" suit would not be of the Sears and Roebuck variety.

After supper, seeking some solitude away from the family (some of whom still appeared to be recovering from their earlier illness), I went upstairs to my room. I was rummaging through an old apple box of toys salvaged from Sundquist's dump when I heard Ma searching through Dave and Odin's bedroom. As she left the room and started downstairs, I caught a quick glimpse of something brown draped over her arm.

Later that night, Ma called me downstairs. I could see that preparations were being made for weekly baths. Pa had set the wash tub in the middle of the kitchen floor, and a large kettle of water for the bath was being heated on the wood-fired cook stove. The wash tub consisted of a galvanized steel tub about three feet in diameter and eighteen inches tall. Because filling and emptying of the tub had to be done by hand, this task was not repeated between the bathers, at least for the younger kids. There was an order of bathing from oldest to youngest, with the youngest not cognizant of the fact they were bathing in someone else's water. When you are eight years old you have not yet learned to recognize the sheen of an oil slick upon the water.

Ma called me away from the kitchen to the living room. In the living room I caught sight of a pair of brown pants draped over the arm of the davenport. "I want to see if Odin's tweed suit will fit you," Ma said as she motioned me closer to the light of a lamp. I looked at the brown tweed pants and then at Ma. They were the ugliest pants I had ever seen. Ma picked them up by the waistband, held them against my waist, and assessed the fit. The speckled brown pants hung down my skinny legs, covering my bare feet and extending onto the floor. Not only were the pants ugly, but they were enormous! Relief began to replace dread as Ma set them aside and looked at me.

I shrugged my shoulders and smiled at Ma, considering myself lucky to be too small for those dreadful tweed trousers. I was about to turn away when Ma's next words stopped me in my tracks. "Take off your pants and try these on."

"W-w-what?" I stammered.

"Try them on," Ma repeated.

She couldn't be serious, I thought. How could she be serious? The pants were huge, enormous even. It would be like trying on a tent. "Oh, Ma," I pleaded, "I can't wear those."

"I'll make them fit," Ma interrupted. "Just try them on, and I'll make some alterations."

Just then, Pa appeared in the doorway, so I hastily removed my Roebuck jeans and awkwardly squeezed my bare leg into the tweed pants. I stood there, shocked and paralyzed as my leg experienced the misery and torture of wool tweed fabric. "Ouch! Oh, ouch, ouch!" I screamed.

"For land sakes, what's the matter now?" Ma snapped.

Whenever Ma was exasperated and needed a phrase to add emphasis, she had her go-to list: "For land sakes," "Heavens to Betsy," and "Good night, Irene." These phrases could be used interchangeably.

"They're scratchy and pokey!" I wailed.

"You'll get used to them," Pa assured me, "and they'll wear like iron."

I had no doubt about the durability of the fabric, but I had concern for the devastation these "wear like iron" pants would inflict on my tender legs. With both legs trapped inside the dreadful tweed pants, doubling the agony and suffering, I stood there like a mannequin while Ma folded up the cuffs and pinned them in place.

"There," said Ma, "that looks just fine, and I can have them ready for you to wear to meeting tomorrow morning."

"The waist," I argued, "it's way too big. It will never–"

Before I could finish my sentence, Ma grabbed a handful of tweed from the area of my backside, gathered it up, and pinned it in place. I looked over my shoulder at the seat of my pants and noticed that the two back pockets now merged in the middle of my bottom. About that time, Dave walked by and took a look at my backside. "You'll either have to make the pockets smaller or make one big pocket in the middle," he chuckled, swatting at my rear.

"You keep out of this," Ma ordered. When Ma finished adjusting and pinning, I carefully extracted my tortured legs from the awful pants and headed to the kitchen for my bath. Bath sessions had long ended for everyone else, and the water was now unpleasantly cool. This was my reward for being last. After a quick bath I was off to bed. The cold cotton sheets felt as smooth and luxurious as satin as I slipped my abused legs into their soothing embrace.

On Sunday morning, after waking up and rubbing the sleep from my eyes, I lay in bed trying to remember what day it was. As I did so, my eyes followed a dusty shaft of sunlight from my window, which seemed to spotlight something at my bedroom door. There, hanging on a hanger over the top of the door, were the tweed pants along with a matching tweed jacket.

"Andrew," called Ma from the base of the stairs, "get down here. I want to see you in your new suit."

New? I thought to myself. Those scratchy hand-me-downs aren't new. They're as old as the hills. The very thought of them "wearing like iron" filled me with dread.

"Hurry up," called Ma. "I want to see if the jacket needs further alterations."

"Yeah!" hollered Odin from the next room. "Get down there and experience the wonder of tweed on skin!" In many families a comment like this would be considered hurtful, but in the Hale household this was acceptable speech amongst the siblings and was to be understood as a kind of love language. Cursing and immoral speech was strictly forbidden, but all other forms of teasing and colorful language were okay. Pa and Ma refrained from teasing talk, but mostly tolerated it amongst the kids.

There was no escape. I crawled out of bed and stood before the hangered suit. For several minutes, I stared at its awful arrogance, every coarse tweed fiber mocking me with the promise of endurance.

While contemplating my misfortune, Ma appeared at the top of the stairs. "Don't just stand there," Ma said in a conciliatory tone as she took the suit down from its intimidating perch. "You'll get used to it, and you'll look really good in it."

Ma carried the suit downstairs to the kitchen, and I reluctantly followed. By the warmth of the cookstove, Ma watched intently as I solemnly squeezed myself into the miserable pants. Ma handed me a T-shirt, and I pulled it over my head. She adjusted it so that the tag was at the back and helped me struggle to get my arms through the sleeves. Next, I put on a short-sleeved white dress shirt and finally the matching tweed jacket. Ma spent several minutes fine-tuning the fit of the pants, then attached a dark blue clip-on bow tie to my shirt collar, which I was certain I had seen somewhere before.

Thanks to the jacket's thoughtful lining, my arms were shielded from the torment my legs endured. "Why don't they line pants?" I grumbled. "It would make sense." Just then, Odin appeared in the kitchen and gave me a thumbs-up. "Shut up!" I snapped. Mornings were never the best time to humor me.

"I didn't say anything," Odin retorted. Ma gave him a disapproving look, and he retreated to the living room. Odin always had a look that made it seem like he was about to say something, even when he wasn't. This look often got him in trouble with Pa, who had no tolerance for backtalk.

Ma fussed and adjusted the jacket, tugging at the lapels, shoulders, sleeves, back, and tails repeatedly. All the while, I could only think about the scratchy pants. Why weren't pants lined with soft fabric, I wondered? If pants were lined like jackets, my lower limbs could be spared the slow agonizing deterioration they were about to face.

"That's it!" I blurted out. "That's it!"

"What's it?" Ma asked as I hurried toward the stairs to my bedroom.

"Oh, I need to get something," I stammered. "I need to get my Bible for the meeting."

I found what I was looking for in the bottom drawer beneath a pile of gray and red wool socks. In a few swift motions, I removed the tweed pants, slid on my secret remedy, laughed out loud, and hastily put the tweeds back on. I grinned at myself in the mirror, then rushed out of my room and down the stairs, clutching my Bible. Long-legged underwear was invented to insulate legs from the cold, and this particular pair was my own invention to protect my legs from tweed. Yes, this trip to the meeting would be a little warm, but these Long Johns would be lifesavers.

The tweed suit served me well, and I received more compliments than usual at the meeting. The rugged fabric never faltered or showed any signs of wear. Fortunately, scratchy hand-me-downs had a way of motivating growth, and I outgrew the suit as quickly as possible. It should be noted that I wasn't the only family member experiencing a growth spurt. I watched with interest as Batis also outgrew his meeting clothes.

One Saturday evening, as everyone finished their dessert, Ma informed Pa that Batis needed a new meeting suit. Batis, still licking the last remnants of tapioca pudding from his bowl, pretended not to hear, but I could tell from his widened eyes and paused tongue that he heard every word. He anxiously awaited Pa's response. Sensing an opportunity, I leaned toward Batis, patted him on the back, and whispered something I had been waiting to say for a long time: "THEY'LL WEAR LIKE IRON!"

With Reuben for the push and Stephen for the
pull, Sharon enjoys a wagon ride.

—— •♦• ——

CHAPTER 7

A VEHICLE NAMED LOMAC

O wning a company truck was a genuine rarity on Burn Hill, making our farm quite special.

However, the reason behind having a company truck remained a mystery since the Hale family had no evident need for one. We consumed all the farm's vegetable, poultry, beef, and dairy products the farm produced, so the reason we owned a company truck was never clear to me.

Moreover, considering our farm's modest assets, it seemed improbable for us to possess a company truck. Though it would have been impressive if our truck displayed a sign boasting "Hale Farm, Growers of World-Famous Rutabagas," it didn't. Instead, the side of our truck boldly showcased the faded yet distinct word "LOMAC," harkening back to its previous ownership by LOMAC Electric Company.

Lomac was a 1940 Panel Delivery truck, built by Ford Motor Company to the exact size and specifications as the Ford pickup truck, but with the cargo space fully enclosed. The mystery as to why we owned a panel delivery truck was even more of a head scratcher, since we already owned a 1940 Ford pickup. Technically the Ford pickup belonged to Odin, who had an eye for classic design. Odin recognized, along with other car enthusiasts of the time, that 1940 Fords in both car and pickup configurations were most desirable. With a few body modifications and engine horsepower enhancements, these vehicles became the cool hotrods of the era.

Lomac was clearly not intended for family transportation, and due to its enclosed cargo area, was not the most practical farm truck either. However, the cargo area in Lomac proved to be spacious and dry, making it an excellent play area during stormy days when rain pounded on its steel roof. With Lomac as our getaway car, my companion Mutt and I could recreate our own version of "Bonnie and Clyde," albeit without the real Bonnie and Clyde's legal troubles. We would exhilaratingly navigate the old panel truck through the orchard, speeding past the woodshed and racing over the bridge across the creek.

As rain streaked the windshield, obstructing our vision, we raced across the field and maneuvered through the narrow passage between the big birch tree and the barn. Behind the barn, a logging road entered the woods, skirting around a steep hill. Fueled by our bravery and Lomac's resilience, we veered off the road, scaling the hill and descending the other side, swerving around alder trees and plowing through nettles, ferns, and elderberry bushes. All this excitement unfolded while Lomac remained motionless, parked in the grassy orchard.

The experience would have been even more thrilling if I had been able to get Lomac's engine to start. Unfortunately, due to some mechanical issue, Lomac had been inactive for quite some time, resting beneath a cherry tree in the orchard. Though I had peeked under Lomac's hood on a few occasions, my curiosity never led me beyond marveling at the mysterious blackened mass occupying the space between the radiator and the firewall.

Determined, one day I gathered whatever tools I could find—a pipe wrench, pliers, and a claw hammer—and walked up to the orchard. Pulling the lever on the front of the hood, I raised it and propped it open with a bean pole. Upon removing the radiator cap, the apparent problem became evident—the water level was about an inch low. I filled a mason jar with creek water and topped off the radiator before replacing the cap. Sitting behind the steering wheel, I pressed the starter with one foot and the gas pedal with the other. The engine emitted a sound that hinted at a desire to start, but my mechanical instincts told me there were likely additional issues with Lomac beyond a low radiator.

Climbing onto the large bulbous fender, I scrutinized the blackened engine mass, hoping to find a clue. Spotting the dipstick, I pulled it out and wiped it on my pants. After several attempts at locating the elusive hole, I finally managed to reinsert the dipstick. Pulling it out once more, I examined the bottom as I had seen Pa do. "Oh, oh," I uttered, echoing Pa's words when he checked dipsticks. The oil level was indeed about a quart low.

In the pump house, I scoured the surroundings until I found what I was looking for—a two-gallon can labeled "Fuel Oil." Although unfamiliar with fuel oil, I reasoned that "oil is oil," based on the practical thinking instilled in me. Recalling Pa mentioning Lomac burning oil, it seemed logical to use the type labeled "Fuel Oil." Carrying the can to Lomac, I climbed onto its fender, uncertain where to pour the oil. I searched for a cap, lid, or plug and eventually found a stubborn plug. With the aid of a pipe wrench and a hammer, I managed to loosen and remove it. As the rusty brown water gushed out, I realized I hadn't discovered the oil inlet, but I might have stumbled upon the engine problem.

Whispering to myself, "Yucky, yucky," as the rusty liquid streamed down the engine's side and formed a miniature river snaking through the grass, I observed the flow eventually dwindle to an occasional drip before replacing the plug. I then reopened the radiator cap and, after numerous trips to the creek with my mason jar, refilled the radiator with pure, clear water. Confident that fresh water would do the trick, I attempted to start old Lomac again. However, the stubborn old motor still refused to ignite, showing no remote interest in cooperating.

Reasoning that there must be something else amiss, I recalled observing Dave work on his car and understood that diagnosing engine issues involved a process of elimination. While I had eliminated a couple of possibilities, I also remembered Ma's wisdom that if you fiddle with anything mechanical long enough, it will somehow repair itself, even if you don't understand how.

Attached to a small-diameter tube extending from below and leading to a component on top of the engine, I noticed a small clear glass bowl about the size of a lemon. At the bottom of the glass bowl, there was a thumb screw—a clear indication of its designed convenience for frequent removal. Unable to turn the thumb screw with my fingers, I resorted to using pliers. I emptied the gasoline from the glass bowl, wiped away the dirt with my shirt, and meticulously cleaned both its interior and exterior. As I performed this task, I caught a glimpse of the young mechanic reflected in the dirty windshield. I smiled and he smiled in return. "She'll be fixed in a jiff," I assured him, ducking my head back under the hood. I reinstalled the glass bowl and tightened the thumb screw.

Seated in the driver's seat once again, I made another attempt to start Lomac. I pumped the gas pedal and pulled the choke knob out and pushed it back in. However, the engine displayed even less interest in starting than before, seemingly growing more fatigued by the moment.

Kneeling on the fender, I scrutinized the large, blackened engine mass. In contrast, the little glass bowl, now refilled with gasoline, sparkled like a gem. Although the engine's appearance had improved somewhat, its refusal to run persisted. It became increasingly clear that Lomac suffered from a multitude of problems, including a new problem. There was now gas leaking from the engine. "Flooded," I said to the young man in the windshield. I had learned this term watching Dave work on his 1938 International truck.

Resting on the part of the engine that leaked gasoline was a structure resembling a spoutless tea kettle, topped with yet another thumb screw. Considering my newfound confidence in handling thumb screws, I removed it and lifted off the kettle-like apparatus. It soon became apparent that the kettle consisted of upper and lower halves. The lower half contained a large central hole surrounded by a moat of oil. I emptied the oil and, with my shirt already soiled, proceeded to wipe away the remaining residue. After replacing the kettle and firmly tightening the thumb screw, I sat back on the fender, pondering my next plan.

Hearing a car door slam somewhere near the house, I swiftly slid off the fender and peered around the front of Lomac. Pa had just returned from work and was making his way toward me. Casually, I concealed the pliers in my pocket and slipped the hammer and pipe wrench under the seat. "What are you up to?" Pa inquired, smiling as he surveyed the engine compartment.

"Oh, just needed a little water," I replied, sliding the can of fuel oil under Lomac with my foot. "Didn't need much," I added, removing the bean pole and lowering the hood.

"Well, don't start taking anything apart," he warned, his gaze fixed on my blackened hands.

Uncomfortable with Pa present, I decided to give up for the day. The following day, Odin offered to fix Lomac, which sounded promising since I believed I had already resolved most of its issues. I followed Odin to the orchard, where he lifted the hood, and I propped it open with the bean pole. Odin removed the thumb screw and lifted off the kettle-like component.

"All right," he said, stretching over the engine, "let's check the carburetor." With a flashlight dangling from his mouth, illuminating what I assumed was the carburetor, he next did something that was a mystery to me but only involved the use of a screwdriver.

In the 1950s, and likely since the automobile's invention, men and boys prided themselves in understanding, maintaining, and improving automobiles' appearance and performance. Though this passion for cars has faded in recent years, on the Burn Hill farm, it remained an expected rite of passage.

Both Dave and Odin took great pride in their cars. Dave's first car, a 1936 Chevy two-door sedan, wasn't in the best condition when he acquired it. However, through Dave and Odin's persistence, the car received a significant makeover. They moved it to the shade of a cherry tree in the orchard and set to work. Armed with a bucket of paint and two paintbrushes, they transformed the car into a shiny light gray. In keeping with the trend of whitewall tires beloved by car enthusiasts in the '50s, Dave and Odin meticulously applied a four-inch circular band of white paint to each of the four tires. To further enhance the Chevy's appearance, they purchased four large Cadillac hubcaps from Zahradnik's Auto Wrecking, the local auto salvage yard. Although the hubcaps didn't fit Chevy wheels, they were ingeniously secured with sheet-metal screws. The result? A stylish ride!

Lomac was not considered a stylish ride, but learning from Odin, a seasoned expert in all things automotive, would prove beneficial. Considering my limited knowledge extended to opening Lomac's hood, I hoped Odin would impart some of his auto mechanic wisdom.

Curiosity and admiration compelled me to ask, "How do you know what you're doing?"

"Well," Odin began, "it's quite basic. You have intake, compression, power, and exhaust. By combining the proper fuel-air mixture and introducing it to a precisely timed ignition under compression, the resulting power stroke sets the crankshaft in motion, sustained by the flywheel."

I stared across the orchard, unable to utter a word. I felt as ignorant as a fence post. I attempted to commit his explanation to memory, even though I comprehended not a single word. It simply seemed like knowledge I should possess.

"That should do it," Odin declared as he emerged from under the hood. "Eventually, the carburetor may need a complete rebuild, but it'll be fine for now."

Odin opted not to reinstall the kettle-like component. Instead, he climbed into Lomac, settling into the seat.

"Stand back!" he shouted. After a few moments of groaning, the engine suddenly roared to life with a tremendous bark, accompanied by a flame shooting up from the engine. Lomac was running. Odin picked up the kettle-like component and inspected it.

"Needs oil," he remarked.

"It does?" I innocently asked.

"Yeah, it's an oil bath air filter, but we'll add the oil later," Odin replied, placing it near the cherry tree and closing the hood.

"Hop in, let's go for a ride," Odin invited. Lomac lurched and jerked as Odin maneuvered it out of the grassy orchard and onto the gravel driveway. Testing the horn while passing the house, we came to a sliding stop alongside the woodshed. We embarked on several speedy trips up and down the driveway before returning Lomac to its spot beneath the cherry tree.

"What's with the can of kerosene?" Odin inquired, noticing the fuel oil can in the orchard.

"Kerosene?" I stammered, "but it says fuel oil."

"Did you put some in the engine?" Odin continued. "You did, didn't you? You thought it was oil, right? Didn't you notice the kerosene smell?"

"No," I replied, feeling utterly foolish, "I just thought it was regular old oil for motors and stuff."

"Actually," Odin said, "I was planning to add a little kerosene to help free up some sticky valves, so what you did was okay."

That night, Odin discussed Lomac with Pa and Dave.

"The carburetor may need a rebuild, or maybe the float level just needs adjustment," Odin explained.

Wanting to take some credit for fixing Lomac, given that Odin had only spent five minutes on it while I had toiled for several hours, I offer this to the conversation, "The valves are kinda sticky, but with the kerosene I added to the motor, it should be running good in a day or two."

Pa and Dave turned their heads, mouths agape, while Odin stood there, appearing as if he wanted to say something.

He didn't.

Queenie and Reuben ride shotgun, with Andrew at the wheel
of this International truck Dave bought for its parts.

CHAPTER 8

IT WAS RED

When it arrived, it did so suddenly and without warning, much like many events on Burn Hill. This particular event unfolded quickly and caught us off guard. It must have been summertime because the grass in the field stood tall. Pa and Ma were not at home, but at their jobs, and the three oldest siblings, along with the youngest, were also absent. Had Pa and Ma been present, the outcome might have been different, but there was no way of knowing.

There was a noise. Sometimes it seemed distant, and at other times it felt closer. Batis thought it might be a tractor, but our neighbor, Mr. Melum, didn't own a working tractor. We could see his rusty, abandoned tractor beyond the barbed wire fence, sinking into the ground. It had been decades since that old tractor made any sound.

"It could be an airplane," Mutt suggested. But deep down, we all knew it wasn't. We occasionally saw small planes flying overhead since we were close to Arlington airport. In the 1940s, the airport served as a Navy bomber base, protecting the mainland from Japanese attacks. By the 1950s, it was primarily used for civilian aviation, with the old military buildings repurposed for commercial use. On this particular day, Pa and Ma were indeed working in one of these buildings. They were employed at Acme Box and Veneer, a small company that manufactured wooden fruit packing boxes.

Dez was the first to spot it. "It's red! It's red!" he yelled, his high-pitched voice cutting through the throbbing sound in the sky. The thing was a couple of hundred feet above the treetops behind the barn. The pounding noise resonated within my skinny chest and echoed off the barn and house. My instinct was to run for the cover of the woodshed, but my quivering legs felt like lead. I stood frozen in place, unable to move.

The sight in the sky was both stunning and terrifying. I had seen similar things in war comics, but this was the first time experiencing it in real life. The deafening sound filled the air as the object seemed content to remain above our farm, seemingly spying on the terrified kids below. Dez continued yelling, "It's red! It's red!" although stating the color did not seem helpful.

Slowly, my legs regained their function, and I started running in confusion. Initially, I headed for the woodshed, but then changed direction, darting towards the cover of the trees in the orchard. The instinct to hide battled with the urge to observe. Soon, all four of us were running in circles, waving our arms, and screaming.

Although we weren't intentionally signaling for help, the object in the sky seemed to take notice of us and began descending. Panic engulfed us as we transitioned from fearful excitement to sheer dread. Dez stopped screaming, but continued to mouth the words, "It's red, it's red." The color was not my concern—my focus was on the fact that it was descending.

The wild screaming and dancing melted away as soon as it had begun. We now stood silent and subdued, as if subjected to a spell.

While we stood in confused submission, the chickens were having the opposite reaction. Normally docile ground dwellers, the chickens were fleeing the epicenter of this event with record speed. Their low flying style of escape was an awkward combination of wild flapping and scrambling legs. However pathetic their flying style, they were soon out of sight around the corner of the barn.

Our cow had already fled to the far corner of the field, looking as bewildered as a four-legged creature could. Queenie, our dog, was nowhere to be found. The descent of the noisy machine was slow and steady. The grass in the field tossed wildly, then lay flat as the thing settled on the ground.

Now what? The thing had landed, but why? Were we the reason for this unexpected visit? Looking at each other provided no answers. We made a cowardly dash for the house, and once inside, I climbed onto the kitchen counter for a view of the field. The thing was obscured from sight by the woodshed.

Conquering fear requires facing it head-on, so we cautiously slipped back outside. Two men were now walking towards us. If they were to reach us, they would have to cross the small bridge over the creek. However, they ignored the bridge and simply walked through the water without breaking their stride.

I noticed they were wearing calf-high leather boots and what Pa referred to as "tin pants," which had a brownish-green color with oil stains. Heavy red suspenders held up the tin pants, and both men wore brimmed hats. I paid special attention to their attire because, in my young mind, that's exactly how I would dress if I were a man.

Why had they come, and what did they want? One of the men was tall, with a wiry build and a square jaw, while the other was slightly shorter, with a stocky build and a double chin. Neither seemed threatening, but it was still challenging to relax as they approached.

"How are you? What's your name?" The man with the square jaw directed his question at me, likely because I was the oldest of the three boys. "Fine," I automatically replied.

"You live here? What's your name?"

I stammered, "A-a-andy."

"Is this your sister? Are these your brothers?"

"Uh-huh."

"Have you ever seen a helicopter before?"

I hesitated for a moment, then answered, "Uh-huh—I mean no, except in a book."

The men explained that they worked for a logging company, conducting surveys for future logging operations near Granite Falls, a small town less than ten miles east of our Burn Hill farm where our grandparents lived.

"Mr. Melum is a logger," I added, trying to contribute something to the conversation and alleviate my own fear.

"Do you kids want a ride?" A quick glance at my siblings made it clear that the answer was no.

"Yes," I replied. "Do you mean right now?"

"Yeah, if you want to go, we can take you for a quick ride right now. Are your parents home?"

I was prepared to answer, but Mutt waved me off. "Our parents are at the box factory. That's where they work."

"Oh, that, hmm ... well ..." The man with the double chin began his sentence but trailed off. The plan for a helicopter ride was fading.

"Their parents aren't home. I think we should ..." He didn't finish the sentence. The idea of a helicopter ride vanished quickly.

My heart sank. From the moment we spotted the red object in the sky until now, we had experienced a rollercoaster of emotions—curiosity, wonder, excitement, fear, terror, anticipation, and now complete disappointment.

"We can't?" I managed to plead.

"No, without your parents' permission, we have to say no."

The men bid us goodbye, turned, and trudged back through the creek towards their aircraft. The rotors started spinning, the roar intensified into a high-pitched whine, and the helicopter effortlessly lifted off the ground. The grass flattened once again. The red object hovered briefly above the barn before disappearing from sight. We stood motionless until the sound faded away.

When Pa and Ma's car pulled into the driveway in the early evening, we rushed to tell them the story. Amidst the chaotic shouts from all four kids, the word "helicopter" managed to be heard, but our bewildered parents struggled to make sense of the fragments of information.

Pa interrupted the commotion, attempting to bring order to the chaotic narrative. "Hold on a minute. Start from the beginning and tell me what happened."

As the three older kids contemplated how to present the story coherently, Dez eagerly interjected with a helpful detail, "It was red."

Marilyn and Sharon pose for a photo. The tool shed and barn are dwarfed by the huge Birch tree in which I built a tree house and a tree outhouse.

———— ⋅✦⋅ ————

CHAPTER 9

TEMPLETON'S

Templeton's was abuzz on that spring day, surprisingly busy despite the morning drizzle. The multitude of cars and trucks parked outside the popular second-hand store indicated it was the place to be on a Saturday afternoon. I was grateful that Pa had driven Lomac, even though its limited seating forced me to sit on a sack of cow feed in the cargo area. The old panel truck would be perfect for transporting second-hand goods from Templeton's store to the Hale farm.

The gravel parking area in front was dotted with large puddles, and Pa had no choice but to park atop one. To keep our feet dry, we exited through the back door of the truck. Pa and Ma went inside the building while I roamed around, observing the merchandise displayed outside.

The one-story building was crammed with better-quality items, while the overflow of less-desirable stuff was spread out in front and along one side. It was a chaotic display of hardware—a vast, disorganized mosaic. From bed springs to tractor tires, bathtubs to splitting mauls, everything imaginable was on show. The real bargains could be found outside, amidst this inventory jungle. Despite the light rain, people were actively shopping.

A woman in bib overalls struggled to open what appeared to be a rabbit hutch, while her three girls leaned out of the window of a green Dodge flatbed truck, eagerly asking, "Are we getting chickens?"

An elderly man and a younger man examined the rusted buzz saw that Pa and Dave had looked at the week before. The older man remarked, "She's seen better days, but you never know. I reckon she could still buck up a cord or two. Dangerous, though. I never fancied myself with just one arm, ya know what I mean."

A boy about my age inspected an orange and black bike I had previously looked at. The bike had large balloon tires, a chrome shock-absorbing spring in the fork, and even a headlight. Although it looked like the bike had been run over by a truck, neither tire had popped. Apart from a severe twist in the frame, it was in perfect shape. I secretly hoped the boy would notice the damage and lose interest, but he kept gesturing to his dad, who was examining a cream separator. Eventually, his dad approached and quickly dismissed the bike as "junk," echoing the exact words Pa had used the week before.

As soon as the boy left, I picked up the bike, swung my right leg over the bar, and, standing on my tiptoes, straddled the bent and twisted frame. I was relieved the boy's dad hadn't let him buy it. I pedaled away from the shoppers and circled Lomac counterclockwise. The bike's natural direction was left, and I circled the truck three or four times. Once I felt comfortable riding counterclockwise, I attempted a right turn and accidentally collided with the side of the green flatbed truck. I lifted the bike out of a large puddle as the girls in the truck giggled. "Piece of junk," I muttered, turning the bike around and walking it back to Templeton's.

Along the side of the building, away from the snickering girls, I observed all the browsers. It was easy to spot them—those who looked but never bought. "Browsing" was what shoppers did when they had no money, while "buying" was reserved for those who did. The phrase "I'm browsing" served as a humble confession of financial limitations, more palatable than admitting "I'm broke." The store clerk would accept this humble response and move on. I had learned this from observing shoppers at the Five and Dime store in town. I had used the phrase myself on multiple occasions and had been a browser for as long as I could remember.

In contrast, whenever Mr. Templeton asked a buyer, "Can I help you?" they would reply with something like, "Well, I was looking at this post hole digger. One of the handles is a bit sawed off, and there's a drilled hole in it. It's pretty rusty too—must have been left out in the rain for a long time. Not much good for anything anymore. Oh, and someone carved 'George' on the handle, but my name's Hank." By this response, Mr. Templeton would understand that Hank had money and was eager to part with it. The buyer would walk away with a "bargain" and later boast to his neighbor, "Yeah, I just bought a dandy post hole digger. Nothing wrong with it at all. The best ones have one handle slightly shorter than the other; fits your hands better, you know. After digging a few holes, all the rust will be worn off, and it'll look as good as new. It even has a hole for hanging it up. Got it cheap because it says 'George' on the handle, but if it's the George I think it is, he takes real good care of his tools."

On the side of the building, Mr. Templeton had lined up a variety of old, four-legged, cast-iron bathtubs. The ones with rust showing through the white porcelain made excellent watering troughs for cattle, while those in fair condition were often purchased by people installing their first bathroom. Those who had a touch of class would enclose the base of the four-legged tub with plywood, covering it with white linoleum. Such a tub could deceive casual observers into thinking it was a modern built-in fixture.

We didn't have a bathroom in our house. However, Pa had plans to install one and had even bought a real flush toilet from Templeton's a couple of years earlier, anticipating the day when we would have our very own bathroom. In the meantime, the white porcelain toilet, complete with a wooden seat, sat undignified and unused in a corner of the chicken house, collecting dust and droppings from chickens unaware of its purpose.

Personally, I was incredibly curious about its function; and as it turned out, I was the only family member to satisfy that curiosity. The old toilet would have been a fantastic addition to our home, but it didn't officially function in the house until sometime after the Hales had moved from Burn Hill.

Beyond the bathtubs, Mr. Templeton had a forlorn collection of wringer washing machines on display, some in decrepit condition. Looking at them gave me an uneasy feeling—not because of their decaying state but due to the danger they posed to anyone brave enough to operate them.

The ringer washer was undoubtedly the creation of a sadistic inventor. The two rubber rollers mounted above the washing machine were meant to squeeze water out of garments but occasionally squeezed the life out of the operator's arm instead. The ringer washer had obviously been designed before safety regulations, with its revolving rollers just inches away from your fingertips as you fed wet laundry through. Once the victim's fingers were caught by the merciless rollers, there was no escape as the arm slowly disappeared into the machine.

Before horror movies on TV, the ringer washer was the primary cause of childhood nightmares. Yet, there was something intriguing about those moving rollers, tempting you to get as close as possible without getting caught.

"Be careful," Ma cautioned as I fetched a stool to get a closer look at the washing machine and its menacing rollers. I climbed on the stool, determined to examine them.

I picked up a washcloth and playfully snapped it at the revolving rollers. "You'll get caught," Ma warned.

Ignoring her warning, I continued snapping the washcloth, daring the rollers to grab it. The rumbling rollers seemed to taunt, "I'm going to get you," while I repeatedly snapped the washcloth at them, replying, "You'll never get me." A couple of times, the rollers caught just the tip of the washcloth, but I managed to snatch it back quickly. After a while, the rollers grew tired of my game and firmly grabbed hold of the washcloth. I jerked it as before, but the rollers held tight. I attempted another pull, but it was too late—the rollers had already caught my fingers and were rapidly consuming my hand.

The pain was excruciating. I watched in horror as my arm began disappearing into the ringer. Ma noticed what was happening almost immediately, but by the time she stopped the machine, the rollers had swallowed my arm up to my elbow.

The physical trauma was nothing compared to the nightmares that followed. Night after night, the rollers invaded my dreams. Giant rollers crept silently across the field toward our house, growing larger until they engulfed the entire house. I would try to escape, but my movements were agonizingly slow, and I could never quite flee in time. With no child psychological counseling available at the time, I had to find my own ways of coping. This included frequently getting up for a drink of water and sharing a bed with my brothers.

As captivating as the merchandise at Templeton's were the people-watching opportunities. This activity intrigued me since I rarely had the chance to observe people I didn't know. I watched an elderly man, draped in a heavy work coat and carrying a cane hooked over one arm, shuffle through the maze of merchandise. He stopped occasionally to scrutinize items that caught his interest, seemingly in no rush as he meticulously surveyed the abundant array of equipment, machinery, and tools.

The old man spent considerable time examining a large tree-felling saw. The saw measured about ten feet in length and had a handle at each end. I had often heard these saws referred to as "misery whips." I continued watching as he slowly ran his hand down the rusted side of the blade, his gnarled fingers bumping along over the teeth. He tested his grip on the handles and sighted along the length of the saw. I wondered why he was interested in such a large saw, considering he was well beyond the age to operate it. And even if he did purchase it, I pondered who his partner might be to handle the other end of such a massive cross-cut saw.

I spotted his partner approaching before the old man did, prompting me to move closer to eavesdrop on their conversation.

"Remember old Jorgenson and Halverson? How they used to brag about dropping a tree faster than any two men alive?"

"You mean back in '23 when we worked for Hawkin?"

"No, you old coot! Don't you remember back in '17 when you had just moved to the Trafton place, and that big Swede, what was his name, was loggin' the flats?"

"That wasn't Halverson. He couldn't have even carried a misery whip to the tree!"

"No, ya ain't never seen him, then. He could handle a saw alright, and he could cut through a log in short order. He looked slow and had a vacant look in his eyes, but he was a heck of a logger, I tell ya."

"Well, I can tell you it wasn't in the teens fer fact, cuz me and Jessie didn't even start buildin' on the Trafton place until fall of '22, cuz Stubbs and his son-in-law didn't put the bridge over till '20 or '21."

Just then, Mr. Templeton walked by and glanced at the old men and the saw. "Stay out of trouble, boys," he said, patting one of the old timers on the shoulder.

As Mr. Templeton passed, a woman approached him and inquired about two pressure cookers resting on top of an icebox. She wore a dress, a man's coat, and tall green barn boots—an appalling fashion choice, I thought. I was glad Ma never dressed like that. My Ma was a lady who always dressed the part, even when working in the garden or feeding the pigs.

The woman pulled a ragged-edged wool scarf from her purse, folded it into a triangle, placed it on her head, and tied it under her chin. Oh, how terrible she looked. I never cared for those wretched-looking scarves on any woman, despite my sisters occasionally wearing them to school or prayer meetings.

She must be unmarried, I presumed, and perhaps destined to remain so. And if she was married, I bet her husband wouldn't be caught dead in public with her.

"Honey Pie!" called a man carrying a wooden apple box full of canning jars. The woman in barn boots looked up and asked, "Oh, what's in the box, Hubby?"

"A dozen pint Kerr jars," he announced, appearing as enthusiastic as a puppy. "I checked the tops, not a single nick on the bunch."

"Oh, and I found a good pressure cooker," said Honey Pie. "I'll make you all the parsnip soup you can eat."

The two of them walked away, happily carrying their jars and cooker.

Inside Templeton's store, I examined a dozen or so radios. The large wood-cabinet radios, some as tall as a chest of drawers, were all plugged in and broadcasting on different stations. There's a peculiar odor that old tube-type radios emit, once they have warmed up. And with a dozen of these radios all congregated in one area of the store, the odor was potent. It was an intoxicating aroma I enjoyed, maybe for no reason other than my fascination with radios. I had always dreamed of having my own radio, but I understood that the one radio we had at home was already a luxury. Our big, boxy, wood-cabinet radio had likely been purchased at Templeton's.

In 1951, Snohomish County Public Utility District installed power poles to bring electricity to Burn Hill. This luxury provided power to twenty-six homes in the area.

Sometime after that, Pa wired our house for electricity, and sometime after that, we acquired our very first radio. Pa and Ma controlled the programming on the big radio, so the idea of having my private radio was merely a dream. What I truly desired was a multi-band radio, enabling me to listen to mysterious shortwave broadcasts, Morse code, and ship-to-shore messages. I believed that within these rarely explored frequencies, where signals faded in and out, I could intercept secret messages from smugglers and spies.

Several kerosene lamps were displayed on top of the old radios. In fact, the store had numerous kerosene lamps of all shapes and sizes. There were plain, clear glass lamps, some with ornate metal bases, and others adorned with hand-painted scenes, elaborate chimneys, and shades. The shoppers at Templeton's paid little attention to these lamps, and I knew the previous owners were glad to be rid of them. They served as a reminder of bygone days without electricity.

The townspeople and most of the rural folk in Snohomish County had been enjoying electricity for several years. Gone were the iceboxes, wood-burning cook stoves, and kerosene lamps. With the arrival of electricity to Burn Hill, the Hale family slowly began embracing the appliances of the twentieth century. The kerosene lamps would be the first to go. No longer would we endure the constant task of filling lamps with kerosene, trimming wicks, washing chimneys, or tolerating the ever-present smell of kerosene fumes.

I can still recall the first night we had electricity in our home. A single 100-watt, incandescent light bulb illuminated the living room with astonishing brilliance. Pa was rightfully proud, and we kids were overjoyed. Ma, however, felt embarrassed and proceeded to go from room to room with a dust mop, laughing as she swept away the cobwebs that hung from the ceilings, exclaiming in each room, "Oh, what a mess!"

Leaving behind the radios and kerosene lamps, I began to wonder where Pa and Ma had gone. I searched the furniture section and the entire store but couldn't find them. They had come to look for a larger kitchen table, a necessity for our growing family. Even with baby Bits receiving her meals from a highchair, the Hale family required a table that could accommodate nine people.

I eventually found Pa and Ma in the parking lot, where Mr. Templeton was assisting Pa in loading a large table into the back of Lomac. The table was made of blond wood with a red stripe painted around its top edge. On the gravel sat several chairs of the same wood, featuring red oilcloth seats and matching red stripes on each leg.

As Pa and Mr. Templeton turned the table on its side to slide it into the back of Lomac, I spotted something underneath that left me in disbelief. The drive back to our home on Burn Hill would be a happy one. Pa and Ma could now anticipate less crowding around the table, while I couldn't contain my excitement about what I had discovered beneath it. I could hardly wait to reveal the incredible find once the table was situated in the kitchen.

Instead of sitting on the feed sack for the return trip, I opted for the luxury of one of the chairs. I couldn't help but gaze at the treasure trove concealed beneath the large table. It was difficult to contain my excitement, but I had to if I wanted to capitalize on this tremendous discovery.

As we pulled into the driveway, the front door swung open, and Batis and Dez came running out. They immediately rushed to the back of Lomac to inspect the second-hand treasures on board. While they seemed pleased with the table and chairs, I would have to wait until the table was in the kitchen before revealing our incredible fortune.

Once inside, Ma began cleaning the chairs and the table's top while Batis, Dez, and I crawled underneath, so I could unveil the secret. Batis looked at the underside of the table and then at me, his face mirroring the astonishment I had experienced when I first discovered the incredible stash. Batis and Dez sat there saying, "Yi, yi, yi!" The spearmint gum was enjoyable, but it couldn't compare to cloves or Black Jack. Batis found a piece of bubble gum that had barely been chewed, and Dez discovered a gob that must have contained three or four sticks.

It was a Templeton treat, a pleasure we would savor just once, and enjoy it we did.

Pa with the Farmall tractor loading logs via makeshift
ramp onto Dave's International truck.

CHAPTER 10

—— •+• ——

HUNTERS AND GATHERERS

I n a distant time, long before the Burn Hill farm emerged from a dense forest of firs, hemlocks, and cedars, it was Native Americans who roamed these wooded hills. Even a century before the fire that gave Burn Hill its name, the indigenous people inhabited this land. While history has documented the skill of Native Americans as hunters and gatherers, they might have been amazed by the resourcefulness of the Hale family. Our hunting and gathering skills were not passed down through ancestral knowledge but were simply the result of curious and inventive young minds. The townsfolk of Arlington, nestled in the valley below this grand old hill, observed our resourceful lifestyle with skepticism. What did they truly know about the art of hunting and gathering?

Hunting and gathering captivated the entire Hale family, but it was the Hale kids who displayed a fanaticism for it. How else could one explain the actions of Dave and Odin, who collected dried goat droppings? They skillfully transformed them into marbles by painting them with vibrant colors and then sold or traded them to unsuspecting classmates at school. The key objective of this endeavor was to flood the market with these peculiar marbles, selling as many as possible before rain ruined them or before an oblivious child mistook one for candy.

To succeed in this hunter-gatherer enterprise, one must maintain an open mind and embrace nature's offerings whenever they present themselves. Combine this open-mindedness with a touch of boredom, and you have the mental climate in which one gathers just about anything. For instance, it was out of sheer boredom that I discovered the large blobs of yellow jelly that ooze from cherry tree trunks can be an interesting treat—or at the very least, tolerable.

I must admit, I found more success as a gatherer than as a hunter. Hunting demands a keen understanding of animal behavior, a willingness to work hard, and enthusiasm for early mornings—none of which described my approach to life. Gathering, on the other hand, often required minimal effort, and the resources to be gathered were usually easy to find.

However, there were times when gathering nature's bounty became vital for our family's well-being. One such occasion was when Ma announced that the cupboard was bare. With most of our siblings still asleep, Ma asked Mutt and me to go out and gather eggs.

The task of gathering eggs was no longer the responsibly of Dave, Odin or Anne Oakly. These older siblings were now in their teens, and either working away from home or had taken on other responsibilities within the family. Because of this, Mutt and I fulfilled a unique role within the family unit without even realizing it. With three siblings above us and three siblings below us, we had become the bridge between the three who were well on their way to adulthood and the three youngest, who were still learning the responsibilities of life.

On conventional chicken farms, eggs are systematically collected from chicken houses, where hens live structured and orderly lives. As one would expect in such an orderly egg-laying institution, hens line up like dairy cows and deposit one egg each day into little boxes. But on the Hale farm, egg gathering resembled an Easter egg hunt. Our colorful, albeit not exceptionally intelligent, bantam hens laid their eggs wherever the urge struck them. Eggs could be found in the garden, the woodshed, or even on the roof of the pump house, but only if you happened to be there at the precise moment of deposit. If you weren't there, the egg would be discovered sunny side up on the ground.

During our search for eggs that morning, Mutt and I entered the woodshed when she suddenly yelled, "Watch out!" I instinctively ducked, half-expecting something to fall from above. "On the ground," she said, as she swiftly picked up an egg just before I stepped on it. I spotted the next one and climbed onto the woodpile to reach it.

Just outside the woodshed, we discovered that a clever hen had laid an egg in a pan of vegetable peelings left by Ma for the ducks.

We knew from experience that the haymow would be the hot spot for egg gathering. To be safe, we quickly surveyed the pump house roof, fully prepared in case a mischievous hen was contemplating a deposit. In chicken terms, such a deposit is referred to as a "roller."

In the haymow, we found seven "droppers"—eggs that had been laid from the lofty height of a rafter tie, falling a mere eighteen feet. Droppers could be divided into two categories: Grade A, which landed in a soft cushion of hay, and those that hit the floor, which were not usually considered for grading.

With three eggs from the woodshed, one from the peelings pan, and five Grade A droppers from the haymow, we had gathered nearly enough eggs for breakfast. Upon returning to the house, we found Batis and Bits eagerly waiting at the kitchen table. Dez was just coming down the stairs from his bedroom with his hair sticking out sideways, dragging a pair of pants by one leg. This sleep-addled figure with a pale face and crusty eyes was a common sight around our place. The Hale family had a name for someone afflicted with this appearance—we called it "stawgna head."

Dez looked blankly at the successful gatherers and took his place at the breakfast table. Gatherers often endured similar vacant stares, as their generosity was rarely acknowledged with even a grunt or a smile. Mutt and I stood there, exchanging a knowing look. A shared understanding welled up within us, unspoken yet profound, connecting us to every gatherer who had ever lived, from an Inca maiden returning to her village laden with a basket of wild currants to enhance another's feast, to a young Tibetan tribesman traversing treacherous mountains in search of firewood for someone else's fire, or a young Native American brave returning wet and tired to his tribe from ancient Burn Hill with six precious grouse eggs nestled in a cedar basket.

That's just the way it is. Throughout the history of human existence, resourceful and diligent gatherers have braved the elements and risked their well-being to sustain and provide for others, even for ungrateful stawgna heads.

With these thoughts swirling in our minds, Mutt and I solemnly presented the only food source available, the one that stood between our helpless siblings and hunger: nine precious eggs. Mutt and I consumed our small portion with a dignity that would have made our ancient ancestors proud.

———— •+• ————

One would never expect to find clams on Burn Hill. Yes, I'm talking about the bivalve creatures commonly associated with the seashore. If you were to bet your wallet that no clams existed on Burn Hill, you should hope your wallet contains no more than two nickels. Surprisingly, clams did exist on Burn Hill, and this phenomenon might yet remain undiscovered by the scientific world.

Batis sat on the bridge that spanned the creek, letting his rubber boot dangle in the slow-moving water. "Get a stick. I see something shiny in the water."

I took a quick look and indeed, there was something shiny in the muddy creek bed. I went to find a stick. Upstream from the bridge, there was an abundance of hardhack growing on each side of the creek. I snapped off a four-foot branch from a bush and returned to the creek. Poking around in the muddy water, I tried to push the shiny object toward the edge of the creek. However, my attempts only stirred up the mud and clouded the water.

"Now you've lost it," Batis protested. "Get a shovel."

We found a shovel in the woodshed and used it to scoop mud from the creek bottom near where we last spotted the shiny object. The shiny thing turned out to be a piece of broken glass, but in the process of digging through the mud we made an unexpected discovery.

Batis held something small on the tip of his index finger. "Look, a baby clam," he said.

"That ain't no clam," I mocked.

"Well, then why is its mouth open?" Batis replied, holding his finger close to my face.

I stared at the tiny creature on his finger. "That can't be a clam because clams only exist in the ocean."

Batis once again brought the clam near my face, and this time the clam had closed its mouth.

Digging deeper into the mud, we found more of these tiny clams. They were no larger than a baby's fingernail and about the same color.

"Will they get bigger—I mean, so we can eat them?" Batis asked. However, these tiny bivalves would need to grow significantly before we could even consider them for a meal. It would require a thousand of these tiny clams to make a single bowl of chowder.

We found a two-pound Folger's coffee can in the pump house, which would serve as the home for two dozen clams for the next few months. We filled the can with mud and placed the tiny clams on top. We kept the can by the creek.

"I think they'll get bigger," I said confidently.

The next day, we checked on our baby clams.

"The clams are gone. A bird must have eaten them," Batis lamented.

Before dumping the mud from the can, we gently probed the surface and discovered that all the clams were just beneath the surface of the mud.

The clams thrived in the coffee can throughout the spring, summer, and into the fall as we waited for them to grow.

Grow, they did not.

———— •+• ————

Spring rains bring forth an abundance of wild plants, some of which I found enticing enough to gather for their culinary appeal. Most of these plants wouldn't meet Ma's standards for the dinner table, and certainly would not be found in A Field Guide to Edible Plants of the Northwest. However, it's important to note that the edibility of any plant should be determined by the individual, not by some nature author with a PhD in horticulture. Now that I've clarified this common misconception, I can proceed without apologies.

"Shh," Batis motioned, placing a finger to his lips. "Someone's in there." Batis and I were positioned directly behind the outhouse—a two-hole structure most family members simply referred to as "the toilet." Our purpose for lurking near this despised outbuilding was to gather the most delectable leaves of sour junk we had ever come across. Sour junk, as we called it, is more formally known as sheep sorrel—a low-growing weed with arrow-shaped leaves featuring distinct horizontal lobes at the base. Sour junk had a flavor reminiscent of sour pickles, and while it couldn't be considered a complete meal, it did serve as a treat until Ma called us in for lunch or supper. The leaves we sought were typically around two inches long, but behind the outhouse, they grew to an astonishing length of four inches.

The Hale kids were never deprived of food, as Ma always managed to provide a tasty and satisfying meal for the family. However, due to financial constraints, treats were a rarity in our household. Sour junk was a treat.

Receiving store-bought treats wasn't a common occurrence for the Hale kids. It's likely most people wouldn't remember their first ice cream cone or potato chip, but I remember both.

My inaugural ice cream cone was savored while riding in the back of our 1940 Ford pickup truck. Ma had driven the old truck to town to fill the water tank that occupied most of the space in the back. There was just enough room for Mutt, Batis, and me to squeeze in around the water tank for the ride.

Before heading home with a full water tank, Ma made an unexpected stop at the little store across from the high school on French Street. To our astonishment, she purchased ice cream cones for us. We eagerly enjoyed this treat on the journey home, although it came with significant challenges. The combination of a scorching summer day and the turbulent airflow in the back of the truck caused our treats to rapidly melt, splattering bits of ice cream all over us, the truck, and the water tank. It was a messy yet delicious predicament!

Potatoes had long been a staple on American dinner tables, but they only became a treat after the invention of potato chips in 1853. Now, almost a century later, a bag of potato chips made its debut in our Burn Hill home. This treat wasn't purchased by our parents but by Dave and Odin, who seemed to have some disposable income. The potato chips weren't meant to be shared, but since I couldn't resist begging and my mouth was watering, they gave me one large chip. To this day, my favorite treats remain ice cream and potato chips.

Sour junk couldn't be compared to the likes of ice cream or potato chips but given the scarcity of store-bought treats in our home, sour junk would have to suffice. To be honest, sour junk wasn't a spectacular treat, but it was a treat nonetheless, and it didn't cost a penny to gather.

As to why sour junk thrived so abundantly behind the outhouse, I can't say for certain. However, looking back on it now with some horticultural knowledge, I hope it was due to the area being shaded from the afternoon sun rather than any fertility advantage.

The sound of shuffling feet coming from within the outhouse was interrupting our snacking on sour junk. "Who's in the john?" I whispered, using a less formal term I preferred over the word toilet.

"It could be Pa," Batis suggested. We silently retreated from the back of the outhouse, crouching amidst the weeds, tall grass, and sour junk.

"It's not Pa," I whispered. "I just know it's not Pa."

"How can you tell? Can you really tell?" Batis questioned.

"Because," I explained, "I can hear someone on the small hole." The outhouse was conveniently constructed with a larger hole for bigger bottoms and a smaller hole for smaller ones.

"In that case, it's probably Dez," Batis whispered mischievously.

"Should we dare peek through a knot hole? What if it's Pa? He'll be super mad," I cautioned.

"Hey, you said you heard someone on the small hole. If someone's there, it can't be Pa," Batis explained. Batis had a way of laying it all out in simple terms that seemed so logical that you'd have to be crazy to question it.

"Yeah, but what if ..." I began, thinking I had discovered a flaw in his logic. However, before I could fully process it, we heard a muffled cough emanating from inside the outhouse. Suddenly, I couldn't recall the flaw I had detected; and besides, the cough sounded just like Dez.

"That's Dez," I said. "For sure, it's Dez."

Batis reached back and plucked a two-foot stem of timothy grass, complete with a bushy seed head, and handed it to me.

"Okay then," Batis whispered through clenched teeth. "Stick it through that knothole right behind where Dez is sitting, and if it's him, he'll yell."

Once again, it was hard to argue with such straightforward reasoning. I took the stem of grass, inserted the end with the seed head through the knot hole, and wiggled it around. Nothing happened. As I was about to pull the stem back out, we heard the creak of the outhouse door opening and then slamming shut. We fell back, flattening ourselves as best we could amidst the weeds, tall grass, and sour junk—and we waited. After an appropriate amount of time had passed, we cautiously peeked around the corner of the outhouse. Pa was just reaching the back steps of the house.

"I could have told you it was Pa," Batis began. "If Dez had been in there on the small hole, Pa wouldn't have been in there too. And if Pa hadn't been in there, this wouldn't have happened."

That statement was a real head-scratcher, requiring more in-depth calculating of which my brain was not capable. As I gathered a good handful of sour junk and stuffed it into my mouth, I realized I was never good at solving story problems, and I wasn't about to let this one ruin my entire day.

———— •+• ————

There is a trick to gathering and eating nettles. These plants are notorious for their painful stings on human flesh. However, it was precisely because of their stinging nature that we became intrigued with finding a way to eat them without getting stung.

One Sunday afternoon, Pa and Ma took us kids to visit our cousins in the small town of Granite Falls. On previous visits, my cousins always made an effort to demonstrate their superiority in everything from sports to worldly knowledge. This time, I was determined to show them that they weren't as great as they thought.

While Pa, Ma, and my siblings went into the house, I headed straight to the woods with my twin cousins, Joey and Jimmy. There was always a friendly rivalry with our cousins, so I had a little surprise in store for them.

Behind their house, in a wooded canyon, I found a large patch of nettles. I promptly picked a big nettle leaf and folded it in half. I held it up so that Joey and Jimmy could fully appreciate its deadly potential. Satisfied I had their full attention, I took a daring bite out of the leaf, chewed it up, and swallowed it. Joey and Jimmy stood there bewildered, their eyes wide and their jaws dropping to the ground.

"Nothin' to it," I said, spitting out a stream of nettle juice. "I bet you guys can't do it. I bet you can't eat a nettle leaf without getting stung," I taunted.

"Yeah, well, there must be some trick to it," Joey replied, neither admitting defeat nor accepting the challenge.

"Well, you saw me do it with your own eyes. If you guys are as smart as you think, eat one yourselves," I continued.

Playing around with stinging nettles obviously made my cousins nervous, and I noticed Jimmy starting to back away. Sensing a possible admission of defeat, I picked another large nettle leaf and issued a new challenge.

"Okay, here's the deal, if I take a bite out of this nettle leaf and don't get stung, will you guys do it too?"

"Yeah," Joey said, not wanting to seem weak, "but only if Jimmy does it too."

I slowly folded the leaf in my fingers to further enhance their bewilderment, and with a quick, vicious bite, I rapidly chewed it up and swallowed it.

"Aha," Joey shouted, stepping forward. "I can do it, cuz I just figured out how you did it. You just chewed it up so fast it didn't have a chance to sting you."

I carefully selected two small leaves from the top of one of the venomous plants. Folding the leaves in half, I handed one to Joey and one to Jimmy. My cousins stood there, half-paralyzed, staring at the leaves.

There was a clever deception at play in this nettle-eating adventure. Nettle leaves have stinging hairs on the underside. The large leaves taken from lower parts of the plant have almost no hairs, while the small leaves at the top are loaded with wicked stinging hairs.

My cousins had not been educated about this scientific tidbit, but they were about to learn it firsthand.

"On your mark!" I shouted, hoping to proceed before they had a chance to back out. "Get set!" I blurted hurriedly, as Joey and Jimmy exchanged nervous glances, resembling convicts facing their executioner. "Go!" I shouted, clapping my hands together with a pop that sent them into action.

Joey and Jimmy jammed the nettle leaves into their mouths and began chewing frantically. The chewing immediately turned into the most violent wailing and screaming I had ever heard. They spat and gagged, their legs flailing in an uncontrolled dance of jerks and skips. And then, like two scalded dogs, they vanished out of the canyon, running back to their house.

I remained in the woods until Pa arrived. My own wailing sounded like a baby's whimper compared to the ear-piercing screeches that had echoed through the canyon just minutes before.

———— ·+· ————

City folk would be hard-pressed to identify a cascara tree in a line-up of native flora. But to a country boy, not only would identifying a cascara tree be academic, but the whys and wherefores of its commercial value could be acceptably articulated. City folk reading this story will, for the present, remain ignorant as to the significance of this marvelous tree; suffice to say that country folk gather its bark, dry it, and sell it for profit.

"Timber!" I yelled, as I tossed the heavy double-bit axe to the side and dove out of the way of the falling cascara tree.

"Whew, almost nailed me," I whispered through a face full of sticks and leaves.

"Ya didn't notch it right, ya dope!" Batis yelled.

The twenty-foot tree had fallen against an ancient cedar stump with a huckleberry bush growing out of its top. It had fallen a full 180 degrees from where I had intended, but the notch was perfect, that I could prove. I had carefully carved the notch in the side of the tree to the direction I wanted the tree to fall, just like Pa had taught me. But despite my careful planning, I couldn't argue with the fact that the tree had fallen in a place that was going to make peeling its bark a much more difficult task.

"Must've been a gust of wind," I muttered while plucking a twig from my ear.

"No, it wasn't a gust of wind," Mutt countered, "it was just a stupid axe job."

Her words hung in the humid air for a moment then stung like the slap of a willow branch across the face. I walked away to retrieve the axe and to allow time for the hurt to subside.

There were woodsmen who worked these forested hills who could set a stake in the ground a hundred feet from a mammoth Douglas fir tree and watch the stake be driven into the ground just seconds after yelling "Timber!" I wanted more than anything to be a capable woodsman who could handle an axe, stroke a big crosscut saw, and drive a felling wedge with a ten-pound maul.

I could remember seeing Pa walk up to a giant fir tree and study it for felling. With an arm extended and a double-bit axe dangling like a pendulum from his hand, he sighted up the tall tree to check its plumb. Stepping back from the tree, he would remove his cap and wipe a sleeve across his forehead while he studied all the surrounding trees. Satisfied that he understood what tactics the big tree would allow and what path it would descend through the surrounding trees, he proceeded to carve the all-important notch. The chips that flew from the business end of his razor-sharp axe were as big as saucers and shot away as if exploding from the tree. The science of the notch was something Pa had mastered. With the all-important notch completed, he then moved to the other side of the tree and made what he called a back cut with a one-man cross-cut saw. With the final stroke of the saw the tree had only to await the command that all trees understand.

"Timberrrr!"

With orders received, the big old tree would obey and begin its whispering descent while all the surrounding trees seemed to bend slightly out of its destructive path. The thundering sound that was heard and felt when the giant tree met the ground was an ovation for Pa. A job perfectly done.

Someday I'll be a woodsman too, I reasoned. And someday my brothers and sisters won't mock. I was still musing about my someday fantasy when I sensed something moving in front of my face. It was a gloved hand waving close to my face.

"Hello, hello!" a voice echoed. I recognized the voice as that of one of the mockers. "Are you going to help peel this tree or just stand there dreaming?"

I picked up the axe and with two hands threw it as hard as I could at the big cedar stump. The head of the axe buried itself deeply into the moss-covered ground several feet to the left of the stump. I looked at the base of the cascara stump and at the pile of dime-sized chips produced by my axe work and kicked them in disgust.

"Git yer knife out," Batis snapped. "Cuttin' down a tree is the easy part. Peeling this thing all stickin' up in the stump and huckleberry ain't so easy."

My knife, now that was a piece of equipment with which I was no slouch. Just one look at the knife and you would understand that this knife was for very serious work. The unglamorous knife had a mean-looking foldout six-inch blade and had that no-nonsense appearance that only a boy pretending to be a man could truly appreciate. The bulky knife was of very stout construction with not a bit of fancy bone or plastic to cheapen its deadly appeal. On the back side of the handle hinged a deadly looking six-inch spike, the purpose of which I hadn't a clue. The knife came to be in my possession through the fortunes of an astute trade that I pulled off with a kid at school. The kid ended up with a black rock with silvery flecks that I called a meteorite and I walked away with what he called a Russian army demolition knife.

"Are ya just going ta stand there with your dumb knife or are ya going ta help us peel some bark?" The mocker was obviously not familiar with Russian craftsmanship.

"OK," I said, "I'll show you what this dumb knife can do," as I rapidly sliced a large strip of bark from the tree.

Batis and Dez had already stripped several pieces of cascara bark, and Mutt was busy stuffing the bark into one of three gunny sacks we had brought for that purpose.

Using the point of the Russian demolition knife, I made several long incisions up the trunk of the tree. By spacing the incisions about three inches apart and then using the mysterious spike on the back of the knife, I was able to slip the strips of bark off the cascara tree with incredible speed.

I was almost certain someone would comment on the skill and speed with which I handled the big knife, but no one seemed to notice. In fact, the peelers seemed to be doing their best to look the other way.

"Boy," I said finally, "it sure pays to have the right tool when doing a job, doesn't it?"

The peelers hunkering over the fallen cascara tree didn't look up or say a word. It was as if my words had immediately dropped off the edge of the earth. It's so hard to get a compliment when you desperately need one.

"Ya know," I said, aiming my voice directly at the three peelers, "no matter what kinda work a guy does, he's gotta have the right tool." A subtle comment to be sure, but one that should draw the attention of these unskilled peelers to the master in their midst. After suffering the rudeness of a few more minutes of silence I continued, "But then, even with the best of tools it takes an expert to really do a quality job."

It seemed that finally a response was forthcoming as Batis had stopped his peeling effort and was looking rather intently at my big Russian demolition knife. I waited.

"Hey, does cascara really work?" he asked.

"What's it supposed to do, anyway?" Dez piped in.

"It makes a person go who can't go," Mutt replied.

"That's crazy," Batis chuckled. "If ya gotta go ya just go. Who ever heard of a person needin' something to make 'em go?"

"Well, it's true anyway," Mutt continued. "Certain people have problems, and cascara medicine makes the problem go away."

"It must work pretty good," Dez said, "cuz people pay good money for it."

"That don't mean nothin'," Batis argued. "People pay good money for lots of stuff that don't work."

"Like what?"

"Well, like Fords and Studebakers and Plymouths; people pay lots of money for them and they don't work."

"Well, they work sometimes," I interrupted, "but cascara works every time."

"How do you know, Cramp?" Batis growled.

"'Cause one time I licked the sap off the back of some bark, and it made me have the trots."

"Just by licking the bark ya got the runs?"

"Yep, just by licking the bark I got the runs!"

Batis seemed highly amused by my experience and howled with laughter.

"It was probably from eating too many prunes," Batis snickered.

"No, it wasn't prunes, it was cascara. And if ya don't believe me just lick some and find out for yourself."

Before I had finished my challenge, Mutt pulled a foot-long strip of bark from the gunny sack and held it out to Batis. Batis grabbed the strip and proceeded to lick all over the slippery underside of the bark. He then sat back against an alder tree and waited.

"Nothin'," he said. "Nothin', nothin', nothin'. It just don't work."

Mutt handed him another strip and he promptly licked up all the sap. Moving over to the gunny sack, Batis nonchalantly licked five or six more strips of bark.

"Lick-nothin', lick-nothin', lick-nothin'," he chanted as he licked and tossed each strip.

"It just don't work," he stated flatly when he was finished. "Let's just finish peeling this tree, haul the bark to the barn, hang the strips in the haymow to dry and be done with it."

"Then we'll sell it," Dez exclaimed.

"Yeah," Batis blurted, "we'll sell it, and when it's finally mushed up and put in a bottle and sittin' in some store, someone will pay good money for it, and it won't work."

He was right, of course. This cascara didn't seem to be working, at least not for Batis, and he had licked enough cascara to loosen up a horse.

In about two hours, we were finished with the tree and except for the smallest branches, we had the entire tree stripped of all its bark.

Arching kinked backs and stretching cramped legs, we took a few moments to survey the scene of our accomplishment. The naked form of the medicine tree now provided an element of vivid contrast to every other texture and color in the woods.

"It's kinda pretty, ain't it?" Mutt said as she stared at its slippery and pale form displayed against a backdrop of velvety moss and the blackened hulk of the ancient cedar stump. The scene provided a deep sense of satisfaction that only a fellow gatherer could appreciate.

I wiped the big blade of my Russian demolition knife on my pants, snapped closed the blade and spike and stuffed it into my pocket.

"Yup," I said, "it's real pretty."

"Two gunny sacks full and one almost full," Dez announced as we gathered up the three sacks and other equipment for the trek home. Grabbing one of the sacks of bark and leading the way, Batis chuckled.

"So, people pay good money for this stuff, and it don't work."

"Well, it worked for me," I replied. "Maybe medicine just doesn't work on you."

"Guess not," Batis called gleefully as he high-stepped his way through an area of tall ferns.

Suddenly his high-stepping abruptly stopped. Turning slowly around, he stared into my eyes with a look that could only be described as a combination of terror and disbelief.

"Oh," he said softly.

"Oh, what?" I asked, "What's yer problem?"

"Oh," he repeated while slowly lifting a leg, "oh, it works."

To which Mutt replied, "And that's why people pay good money for it."

Sharon, Reuben, Marilyn, Stephen and Andrew gather before bedtime on the davenport for a hymn sing. Marilyn, always the consummate and patient teacher, helps her younger siblings learn the words and the tune.

CHAPTER 11

BLAME IT ON THE BIG HILL

To anyone living in the great Northwest, stumbling upon a patch of native bracken ferns would be a most ordinary occurrence. However, for Batis and Dez, discovering a large patch of dead, dry ferns on the big hill behind the barn was an exciting find. Although Batis was sometimes called "Nature Boy," the discovery of these dead ferns was of no botanical interested to him. It was the fact that the ferns were dead, brown, and crispy that lit the fuse of his country-boy enthusiasm.

During the previous spring and summer these ferns had grown tall, green, and lush. While still standing tall, these ferns had completed their cycle of life, and were now dead, dry, and seasoned to a golden brown.

"Hey, Cramp," Batis called, as they came running from the direction of the big hill. "You know what we found up on the big hill?"

"You haven't been digging up any graves, have you? Each rock up there marks the spot where one of our pets is buried, and I'll know if you've been digging around any of 'em."

"Hey, just cool it, man. We ain't been digging up any pets," Dez assured me.

Batis stuck his thumb in his jeans pocket, pulled it open, and motioned me to take a look.

"Man, where did you get those?" I whispered in awe.

"We already told you, up on the big hill, and there's lots more," Dez replied, revealing a pocketful of his own.

"Wow," I blurted out, "those are huge."

"Shh, keep your mouth shut, or someone will hear us," Batis warned.

Just then, we noticed Ma standing just fifteen feet away, holding a pan of vegetable peelings intended for the chickens. A sense of guilt overwhelmed us, and we stood frozen, like mannequins, avoiding eye contact.

"So, what's going on here?" Ma questioned, scanning each of us with suspicion.

"Nothing," we chimed in unison.

"Well, you all look guilty about something," Ma observed.

That evening, supper proceeded smoothly. The corn casserole, meatloaf, and even the rutabagas went down without complaint. We knew better than to provoke Ma, who already suspected something. The three of us who shared the secret of the ferns remained silent throughout the meal. Ma watched us closely but refrained from commenting. As we left the table, Annie Oakley seemed to sense that something was up and stared at us intently.

"That was weird," Batis remarked once we were outside the house and out of earshot. "Did you see the way Annie Oakley looked at us? She sure thinks she's somebody. It's like having a schoolteacher living with us and watchin' everything we do."

The three of us made our way to the barn and away from scrutinizing eyes. Batis and Dez proudly displayed their collection of dried fern stems. These brown stems, slightly larger in diameter than a pencil, had been broken into four-inch lengths. We climbed the stairs to the haymow and proceeded to the open haymow door that overlooked the big hill and the woods beyond.

Smoking a dried fern requires a certain technique. Ferns burn fiercely, and due to their porous interior structure, hot gases, glowing charcoal, and flames pass through without resistance. Puffing on a fern with too much force invites the flame into your mouth. This does little to maintain the health of one's taste buds, tonsils, and vocal cords. Batis handed us each a handful of wooden kitchen matches, and I struck one against the zipper of my jeans and cupped the flaming match in my hands to protect it from the breeze.

I looked around to see if my brothers appreciated my style, yelling "Ouch!" as I dropped the burning match from my scorched hand. I quickly stamped it out and tried another. Lighting a fern is akin to lighting a firecracker—you want to keep a safe distance once it ignites.

After a few cautious drags on the fern, I began to find the right balance of suction without drawing fire into my mouth. Smoking a fern requires constant vigilance. While not as dangerous as smoking a firecracker, it presents its own challenges.

"Check it out!" Batis shouted, pointing at Dez, who had something similar to a forest fire burning in front of his face.

"How did you do that?" I asked in disbelief.

Dez removed the burning mass from his mouth and replied, "Three at once." Despite his slightly blackened face and charred eyebrows, he seemed unharmed.

Batis and I chose to overlook Dez's lack of finesse in smoking, considering his limited exposure to smokers. In fact, none of us had encountered many opportunities to observe smoking since we grew up in a non-smoking family.

From my limited observations, I noticed that smokers not only mastered the act of inhaling and exhaling smoke but also exuded a certain style—a coolness that made smoking appear macho. I was aware that the art of smoking involved an intangible quality, a look that conveyed casual confidence.

Batis had already come to some conclusions about looking casual and was working on his style. I watched him in the dim light, as he stood leaning against the frame of the open haymow door, his thumb hooked cooly into a belt loop, while a flaming fern dangled loosely from two fingers. His eyes penetrated the country beyond the mow, and he occasionally flicked a burning ember from his fern. I knew he would say something, so I waited.

"Yup," he drawled, "I got me a good smoke and a good place to smoke it. A man can't ask for much more than that." Very impressive, I thought.

As I adjusted my posture to mimic a gunslinger—feet wide apart, slightly bent knees, and a subtle tilt at the waist—I completed the look by casually placing my hand in my back pocket. With a blazing fern dangling from my lips, I searched for the appropriate words.

"Yeah, I've smoked worse," I lied. "City folks would pay good money for—" Just then, a chunk of glowing charcoal fell from my fern onto my flannel shirt. I nonchalantly flicked it away with my index finger, sending it spinning out of the haymow. It was a smooth move, if I say so myself.

"Yeah, they would," Dez chimed in. "They'd pay a pretty penny for smokes like these."

Despite our beginner status, we were doing well in the image department, striking macho poses, puffing on our ferns, occasionally flicking off ash, and extinguishing the burnt ends. However, we were struggling with conversation, realizing that repeating, "Yup, these are good smokes" would sound silly after a while. I could sense that if we didn't find a mature topic to discuss soon, one of us would burst into laughter, ruining the act. That's when I recalled an adult topic I had heard Pa discussing with Uncle Percy, and I wasted no time bringing it up.

"What do you think about Japan?" I began.

Dez, fixated on the burning end of his fern, replied without looking at me, "Why should we care about Japan?"

Perfect, I thought to myself. "Well," I said, casually flicking away a piece of charcoal, "we pretty much wiped them out in the war. I mean, what are they going to do to make a living?"

Batis pondered for a moment, taking a slow drag on his fern. "Seems like they'll just keep making toys and little plastic gizmos for cereal boxes."

Dez struck a match, preparing to light another fern. "Seems to me they can just keep on making a living selling keychains and chopsticks?"

As Dez finished speaking, there was just enough flame left on the match to light up. He gave us a little time to admire his act and then continued, "They can't make quality stuff. Remember that cheap cardboard guitar Odin got for selling seeds? It had 'Made in Japan' written on it."

"Wait a minute," I interjected, stomping out a live butt on the floor. "They made more than just keychains and chopsticks during the war. They made tanks, planes, and ships, right?"

"Yeah, Cramp, they did," Batis argued. "But you know, the stuff they make in Japan is not quality like in the United States." Batis took a quick puff and continued, "They lost the war because their tanks and guns were junky and so were their ships and planes."

"Well, ya know," Dez added, kicking a couple of fern butts out the haymow door, "you can even tell by their toys that they don't make quality stuff. Cramp, you even have a tin toy truck made in Japan, and when you look inside you can still see where it says 'Folger's Coffee.' They made that toy out of an old coffee can."

"Yeah," Batis laughed, tossing the remainder of his fern outside. "If you looked inside the wings of their planes, you'd probably find 'Folger's Coffee', or 'Spam' written in there too."

"You're right," I said, kicking away the remaining evidence of burnt matches, fern butts, and charcoal. "Imagine if they made cars, not toy cars, but real cars you can drive—they'd be flimsy like a coffee can, not solid like a Chevy or even a Ford. They'll never be able to make cars."

Batis chuckled, saying, "That's for sure." We had a good laugh, and after wiping off the soot from Dez's face and rubbing off his singed eyebrows, we left the haymow.

As we strolled up the big hill, continuing our conversation about smoking, Batis declared, "I'll never be a smoker."

"Me neither," I agreed.

"Not me either," Dez coughed. "It makes you feel dizzy and sick inside, and your mouth tastes awful."

Smoking was undeniably bad for you. We had reached this conclusion long before the Surgeon General of the United States made it official.

Near the top of the grassy hill, where the woods closed in on the east slope, there were several rocks of varying sizes marking the graves of deceased pets.

"Who's buried under that big rock?" Batis asked.

I cleared away the long grass around the rock and packed it down. "I think it's Curlibs," I answered.

"Curlibs? Who's Curlibs?" Batis inquired.

"He was a dog," I explained. "I don't really remember him because he belonged to Dave and Odin, probably before we were born."

"What color was he? Was he a big dog?" Dez asked.

"How did he die?" Batis wanted to know.

I knew a certain question would eventually come up, and after a long silence, Batis finally asked, "How deep is he buried?"

"Now, what kind of question is that?" I snapped. "Why does it matter how deep he's buried? We're not going to find out."

"Well," Batis challenged, "you dug up a grave here last summer, didn't you? You can still see the pile of dirt where you were digging."

"Yeah, but that was just a bird, not something as big as a dog," I argued.

"What difference does size make?" Batis retorted, pointing to the hole. "They were both living creatures. They both breathed air, saw the world with their eyes, ate food, and had families who loved and played with them."

"OK, OK," I interjected. "Where are you going with all this talk about their lives and eating and seeing? Besides—"

Dez shook his head and interrupted, "But, Cramp, the reason that bird was in the grave is because you shot it with your BB gun."

"Alright, alright," I said, "I did shoot the bird. I admit it. I shot that bird, but I never expected to hit it. I've never been able to hit anything with that gun."

"Until you hit that bird," Batis and Dez reminded me.

"I shot at that bird so many times, and it just sat there in the tree, staring at me. I kept shooting and missing. I didn't think I could hit it."

"But you did hit it," Batis clarified, "and it died."

"OK, fine," I conceded, "I hit it, but it didn't die right away. Remember how I tried to make it live? But then it just died. You know I felt really bad. I even cried a little." A long silence followed. I still carried the guilt, hoping my younger brothers would understand.

Dez broke the silence, speaking sincerely and sympathetically, "And that's why you put it in a jar, screwed the lid on, and buried it here."

"Alright," I said somberly. "What's done is done. I accidentally shot a bird, I felt bad about it, and gave it a proper burial. That should be the end of it."

"So why did you dig it up?" Batis questioned.

"Well," I stammered, "I guess I just wanted to see what it looked like."

More silence followed. Batis walked over to the big rock, rested his foot on it, and said, "I don't blame you for wanting to see what the bird looked like. I would have done the same thing. After all, it was dead, and it didn't know you were digging it up, so it's okay."

"And I did take the bird's skull to school for science, so it wasn't just wasted," I added.

"Well," Batis hesitated, "I wonder how deep they would have buried Curlibs."

"I don't know," I said, contemplating. "If Pa buried him, it would be six feet deep."

"Six feet underground? Why would anyone bury a dog six feet deep?" Batis wondered.

"I think there's some sort of law about it," I explained. "I've heard people talk about burying things six feet deep, whether it's people, cows, horses, or anything."

"Okay, then," Batis inquired, "what if Dave and Odin buried Curlibs? How deep would they have dug?"

"I'm sure not six feet," I replied. "I'd bet a lot less."

"If it's six feet deep, we won't be able to dig it in a month," Batis reasoned. "But if it's only two or three feet deep …" His words trailed off as he stared into the woods.

Engrossed in our debate, we'd failed to notice the setting sun or the encroaching darkness emanating from the woods. It was a darkness that carried a bone-chilling cold and an eerie fear that seeped into our very souls. Whatever frightful possibilities might be lurking among the trees, we could only imagine.

Before any dire suggestions could be made, we sprinted across the field, heading for the safety of the distant house's light. Once inside, as we slammed the door shut, our terror-stricken bodies experienced a final shudder. The hair on our necks slowly released its grip on our skin, and the fear began to dissipate. As the last remnants of fear flowed out of our jelly-like legs and trickled away from our toes, we calmly roamed the room. No one would suspect that we had just been scared out of our wits.

"What's gotten into you?" Odin quipped. "You look like you've seen a ghost."

"Who, me?" I stammered, feigning innocence. "What ghost?"

Odin pretended as though he hadn't heard, keeping his eyes locked on a Popular Mechanics magazine. I let a few minutes pass and then asked the question, "Who was Curlibs?" Odin's eyes never left the magazine, and in a monotone voice replied, "Why, did you see his ghost?"

Realizing that I wouldn't get any straight answers from him, especially about Curlibs, I had to abandon my inquiries. He was too cunning for that. Nonetheless, I couldn't help but wonder how deep Curlibs had been buried.

"So," Odin finally spoke in the same monotone voice, "you thought you saw Curlibs' ghost, huh?"

"No, I didn't see any stupid ghost," I retorted.

"Well, you're not likely to," Odin stated flatly. "He's buried three feet down with a big rock on top. He isn't going anywhere."

"Thanks," I muttered under my breath. "Thanks a lot."

Stephen enjoys a little fun in the snow. The barn and chicken house can be seen in the background. The Corner of the woodshed is seen in foreground.

CHAPTER 12

———— ·+· ————

UNAUTHORIZED DEPARTURES

"Going somewhere?" Ma inquired as I slipped past her in the kitchen and made my way toward the stairs leading to my bedroom. I glanced at the four-foot alder branch in my hand, then back at Ma.

"I ain't going nowhere. Why do you think I'm going somewhere?"

"Well, it looks like a traveling stick to me," Ma observed, studying me carefully.

"A traveling stick? What's a traveling stick?" I feigned innocence.

"Could it have something to do with the things you bundled up in a dish towel and left on your bed?" Ma questioned.

"Huh, what bundle?" Feeble words tumbled from my mouth before I could conjure a more intelligent response.

"I was just practicing, not running away like you think. Just for fun, you know."

"You mean you bundled up three potatoes, two slices of bread, some dry oatmeal, and a compass just for practice?"

"Well, I wasn't running away, if that's what you think. I really wasn't. I was just seeing how much stuff I could fit in a bundle, just to see."

"And the stick?" Ma approached; her gaze fixed on my eyes.

"What stick?" I blurted, once again displaying my brain's malfunction. "Oh, you mean this stick?" I extended the stick in front of me, pretending to examine it with great confusion.

"Just tell me the truth," Ma insisted firmly.

Attempting to deceive Ma was futile. "Okay," I conceded as calmly as possible. "Okay, I was going to tie the bundle of stuff to the end of the stick and walk around with it over my shoulder, just to see what it would be like."

"And to see what it would be like to run away from home," Ma concluded, finishing the sentence I had started.

With that, Ma walked over to the cook stove, opened the door to the firebox, and threw in a couple of pieces of wood. I felt her eyes on me as I exited the kitchen and slowly ascended the stairs to my bedroom.

"Oh, and by the way," Ma called after me, "when you're done practicing, bring back the potatoes, bread, and oatmeal."

I entered my bedroom and tossed the stick onto the bed. Running away from home wouldn't be easy. I couldn't recall why I wanted to run away in the first place, but I did think it was something a boy had to do to earn respect, especially when feeling undervalued and unappreciated by older siblings.

I wouldn't be the first in our family to run away. Odin had successfully run away a couple of years before. Granted, he had returned, but that's beside the point. The fact was, he had planned it, accomplished it, and when he came back, he was hailed as a hero. He seemed different, more self-assured, and others treated him with greater respect. I could only dream of having such a remarkable runaway story.

When Odin ran away, he hitchhiked his way to the town of Granite Falls, even catching a ride from a police officer in a squad car who assisted him on his journey. Of course, my smooth-talking brother had the officer believing every word he said—where he came from, where he was headed, and the purpose of his trip. It must have been an extraordinary tale that Odin spun, as the officer drove him all the way to Granite Falls and dropped him off in town. From there, the runaway walked a short distance to Grandpa and Grandma Hale's house, where he enjoyed a pleasant visit with them. That evening, Grandpa drove Odin back home. Sure, he hadn't been gone for weeks or months, but he was a bona fide runaway, nonetheless. Ma was upset and a bit teary-eyed, and Pa was somewhat angry. But to us kids, Odin was a hero, like a soldier returning from war. He looked fantastic, even flashing a smile as he was ordered to his room.

Ma's discovery of my ill-conceived runaway notions deflated my enthusiasm. I sat on my bed, contemplating how foolish I must have appeared to Ma, and thinking of all the clever responses I should have given. I knew Ma wouldn't tell anyone, not even Pa. That's just how she was, and I was grateful for that. I only hoped that no one else had overheard our conversation, especially my high-and-mighty sister, the one with the royal blood. It was peculiar that Priscilla had been dubbed Annie Oakley by Dave and Odin, despite bearing no resemblance to Annie in looks or character. Quite the opposite, in fact. Priscilla was the closest a person could get to a big-city girl without actually living in the city. I surmised that she had been bestowed with the name solely to irritate her.

Regarding my runaway plans, I decided to lay low for a while. I knew I wasn't nearly as cunning as Odin and could never make it as far as Granite Falls, but I would run away—my mind was set on it. I just had to be more strategic in my preparations. My pride had suffered a temporary blow, but my determination to run away was stronger than ever.

That night after supper, seeking respite from Annie Oakley's malevolent glances at the dinner table—indicating that she may have overheard my conversation with Ma—I ventured outside. The damp night air provided a refreshing escape from the heat of the scrutinizing gazes I'd endured in the kitchen. Drizzle fell steadily, so I sought shelter in the woodshed. Climbing atop the towering, disorganized pile of firewood, I nestled among chunks of alder and fir. Inside the woodshed, darkness enveloped me, except for a few rays of light filtering through the slats in the walls. There was a wondrous and enigmatic sensation to sneaking away to a place like the woodshed. The only sound was the hushed drizzle, a perfect backdrop for the eerie shadows that materialized, moved about slowly, then vanished into the night.

I rearranged a couple of wood chunks, creating a more comfortable nest, and soon my thoughts returned to my runaway plans. I pondered what it would be like to run away in winter, knowing I would likely encounter rain and possibly snow. Then, a brilliant idea struck me—a stroke of genius that made me smile as the scenario unfolded in my mind. I would run away, but not really run away. Yes, that was it—I would pretend to run away and hide somewhere right on the farm. From my concealed spot, I would bear witness to the weeping, panic, and general hysteria that would ensue once my absence was discovered.

I played and replayed the scene in my mind, visualizing my distraught family scouring every corner of the farm to find me. Each time I imagined it, I added more heart-wrenching details. They would call my name, and some would say, "If only we had treated him better, if only we had listened to his words. He was such a good boy, and we never truly appreciated all that he did for us." I could see their concern escalating from despair to utter panic as they grappled with the dreadful realization that I had run away. The plan was unfolding flawlessly, and I knew it would be a resounding success even before I had finalized all the details.

The woodshed hideout grew cold, and I could smell smoke from the warm fires in the house. Reluctantly, I climbed down from the woodpile and reentered the house. Inside, most family members were engrossed in their evening activities, paying me no mind. Eager to avoid any clever remarks from my older sister, I slipped past everyone and ascended the stairs to my room.

On my bed still lay the bundled supplies for my runaway adventure. Next to the bundle rested a sheet of notebook paper, bearing the words, "THERE WILL BE NO UNAUTHORIZED DEPARTURES." It took me a while to decipher the last two words, but there was no mistaking the author. Only my high-and-mighty sister possessed such elegant penmanship and would use three- and four-syllable words. "Yes, there WILL BE an un-whatever departure," I whispered, crumpling the paper into a tight ball and stuffing it through a knothole in the floor. I knew my sister loved me and was only trying to protect me from myself, but at eight years old, I couldn't fully appreciate this type of affection.

That night, I retired to bed early, lying there in the darkness, contemplating the note. I remained awake for a long time, more determined than ever to execute my runaway plans, if only to demonstrate to my self-righteous sister that I was not her property to rule over. Thoughts of defiance rejuvenated me, and my mind once again delved into strategic planning. I resolved that I would stage my fake runaway on a Saturday when everyone would be home. Right after lunch, I would stealthily slip away from the family. There was a perfect hiding spot beneath a section of the barn floor. This part of the barn had been constructed on posts, suspended over large, ancient cedar stumps, leaving approximately four feet of crawl space beneath the barn floor. Among the old stumps, in semi-darkness, I would have an optimal vantage point of the house and yard. At some point during my plotting, sleep overcame me.

The next morning, I smuggled my runaway bundle out of the house and concealed it inside a hollow stump beneath the barn. Soon, Saturday would arrive, and I would execute my ingenious plan.

As Saturday dawned, I remained in bed, allowing the thoughts of my escape scheme to dance freely within my mind. I had no intention of rising just yet— the house was still frigid. Soon, Pa would light the living room stove and the kitchen cook stove, but I intended to remain nestled under a thick stack of wool blankets until the sound of crackling fires reached my ears. I dozed off for a while and awoke to the comforting symphony of crackling flames and the bustling sounds of kitchen activity. I emerged from my bed, snatched my shirt, pants, socks, and long johns from the floor, and hurried downstairs. Standing in front of the cook stove, I exposed my bare skin to the heat while wafting each article of clothing before the stove before donning it.

"What's for breakfast?" I inquired.

"Oatmeal," Ma responded. "On these cold winter days, you need something to warm you up and stick to your ribs."

Pa stood to the side of the cook stove, engrossed in reading a page from the newspaper he had used to kindle the fire. Buying a newspaper was a luxury we couldn't afford, so Pa retrieved discarded newspapers from town and repurposed them as fire-starting materials. Often, while crumpling up the paper to feed the stove, an article would capture his attention. He would either pause and read it immediately or set it aside for later perusal.

"You're up early this morning," Pa commented without lifting his gaze from the paper.

"I have a busy day ahead, so I thought I'd get up and start," I replied.

It was a foolish response, and I immediately realized my mistake as soon as the words spilled from my mouth. However, when attempting to conceal something, it becomes challenging to provide a smart and articulate answer. Pa merely glanced at me without saying a word.

Before long, the entire family had gathered in the kitchen, passing around a large pot of oatmeal on the table. I helped myself to a second serving. It warmed me up, and as a soon-to-be runaway, I knew I needed something that would stick to my ribs.

That morning, I made an effort to keep to myself. I wanted to secretly gather some provisions for my hideaway beneath the barn. I had hoped to sneak a blanket out of the house, but I couldn't get past the vigilant eyes of those inside, particularly Annie Oakley, my royal-blooded sister.

Nevertheless, I managed to acquire an axe and a coil of rope, which I stashed in the hollow stump where I had previously hidden my runaway bundle. While the axe and rope might not have seemed essential to a runaway, I reasoned that one can never predict what might be necessary.

After lunch, I stealthily made my way into my hideout beneath the barn and settled in, waiting and observing. Soon enough, the family would realize I was missing, and it was that moment of their realization that intrigued me the most. Huddled against the large hollow stump, I sat on the bare dirt ground, shielding myself from the chilling breeze that seeped into my dark and dingy hideout. I was grateful for wearing a wool coat and stocking hat, but I regretted not bringing gloves.

Initially, I didn't spot anyone in the yard, but I could hear Batis and Dez engaged in conversation, likely in the front yard where they were hidden from my view. A little while later, I heard the back door of the house slam shut, and I saw Pa walking through the orchard toward the outhouse. Upon his return, he stopped by the woodshed and carried an armful of firewood into the house. Soon, someone would realize my absence, and the frantic search would commence.

After some time, Dave and Odin emerged from the house and began working on Dave's truck. Dave tinkered under the hood while Odin lay beneath the front of the old 1938 International. Together, they swiftly removed the radiator and placed it on the ground, dedicating considerable time to examining its condition. Eventually, they stowed it in the trunk of Pa's car. Pa joined them outside, and for a while, the three of them conversed by the old truck. I couldn't make out their words, but Dave appeared upset, pacing back and forth and making wild gestures with his hands. "They've realized I'm missing," I whispered to myself. It wouldn't be long before the entire family confronted the heartbreaking reality of my runaway act.

At that moment, Batis and Dez turned the corner of the house and spotted the malfunctioning truck and the assortment of tools. Batis hopped into the cab, pretending to drive and shift gears, while Dez gripped a tool, searching for a place to use it.

"Get away from my truck!" Dave shouted. "And make sure Cramp doesn't touch anything while we're gone!" With those words, Dave and Odin got into Pa's car, exited the driveway, and headed west toward town. Alright, alright, I reassured myself. They haven't discovered my absence yet. But they will, and I'll be right here watching when they do.

Batis and Dez returned to the house, and silence settled in. Shivering in the cold, I tried to curl up even tighter. I pulled the collar of my coat up around my ears, closed my eyes, and attempted to sleep. I wondered about the time, wishing I had a watch or a clock. Though I possessed a compass, it served no purpose in this situation. Why I had brought a compass, I couldn't recall.

During my half-slumber, I felt something cold and wet touch the back of my hand. Startled, I jerked my head up and discovered Queenie standing before me, her curious gaze fixed upon me. Queenie had stumbled upon my hideout and paid me an unexpected visit.

"Are you hungry?" I asked as I reached into the hollow stump and retrieved my runaway bundle. It was unnecessary to inquire since my four-legged friend was always hungry. I untied the bundle, spreading out its contents for Queenie to see the food choices. Before I could stop her, she swiftly snatched up the two slices of homemade bread and devoured them in a couple of loud gulps.

Besides the inedible compass, the remaining items in the dish towel were three potatoes and a loose handful of dry oatmeal. I scolded Queenie, but she attempted to leave. I enticed her back by offering some oatmeal. Splitting the dry oatmeal into two equal portions, I fed her from my hand. In true dog-like fashion, she gagged and sneezed, spraying oatmeal all over me, the dish towel, and the stump. Then, coughing and rubbing her nose with her paw, she promptly departed from my hideout. Queenie paused briefly at the creek, lapped up a considerable amount of water, glanced back at my hideout, and returned to the house.

After Queenie's departure, I did my best to clean up the mess she had created. I shook oatmeal out of my stocking hat, brushed off my clothes, and nibbled on the few flakes that had landed in my mouth. I retied the runaway bundle, which now contained the remaining half portion of oatmeal, along with the three potatoes and the compass. As I contemplated my dwindling food supply, I instantly recognized my sole intelligent food choice had been promptly devoured by a discerning dog, leaving me with three raw potatoes sporting peculiar sprouts, and a handful of dry oatmeal.

Rain began to fall, and the sound of water running off the barn roof reached my ears. I observed no activity anywhere on the farm, nor could I hear any noise from the house. Once again, I tried to sleep, and I believe I did so for an unknown period. When I awoke, I wondered if I might have unintentionally slept through an entire night and part of the next day. The surroundings were exceptionally quiet in the direction of the house. Pa's car was parked beside it. Dave and Odin had returned from town but hadn't resumed their work on the old truck. Presumably, the decision was influenced by the rain, explaining why no one ventured outside. "All the better," I whispered to myself. Since everyone was now indoors, it wouldn't be long before they noticed my absence, triggering the frantic search followed by guilt, remorse, and lamentation.

My thoughts were abruptly interrupted by a loud groaning sound emanating from deep within my gut. The generous helping of hot oatmeal I had consumed for breakfast had just reached its destination in my digestive system, urging me to make a decision soon before the elevator reached the ground floor and the doors opened unceremoniously.

I contemplated making a mad dash to the outhouse, but doing so risked discovery. I surveyed the entire area beneath the barn and settled on a spot in the opposite corner where a couple of stumps offered some privacy. I can't recall why privacy seemed vital, given that there wasn't a human in sight. As I began crawling toward the distant stumps, I suddenly remembered a foolish oversight in my otherwise clever planning. "No paper, no paper, no paper," I groaned. Not a newspaper, not a corn cob, not a leaf—nothing! However, brilliant minds are never stumped for long. Soon enough, I held the dish towel in my hand and crawled desperately to the designated spot in the opposite corner of my hideout. It was precisely at that moment when Queenie reappeared. Dogs possess an uncanny interest in such matters. I commanded her to "go away" and even growled, but she remained steadfast and focused until the elevator scene concluded. Shortly afterward, she left the hideout and returned to the house, briefly glancing back in my direction midway before disappearing. I thought I saw her shaking her head, although I couldn't be certain from that distance. Queenie never returned.

Still, there was no sign of sound or movement from the house, and the lengthening shadows across the landscape indicated that evening was approaching. It was then that I heard the back door of the house slam shut, and I discerned a shadowy figure making its way toward the barn—a figure I recognized as Pa. He carried a swinging kerosene lantern, illuminating his path. I crouched down, watching his approach. Although he couldn't see me, a cold shiver traveled down my spine and fear washed over me, as if the shadowy figure posed some sort of threat to my safety.

Soon, I heard the creak of the barn's side door. The clomp, clomp of boots on the wooden floor grew louder, only ten feet from where I sat in the deepening darkness of my hideout. Through the cracks and knotholes in the boards, faint streaks of lantern light seeped in. There was more clomping, and then the sound of the big barn door opening, followed by the snap of a wire hook holding it in place.

"Come, boss, come, boss," Pa's booming voice startled me, sending goosebumps across my skin. It was milking time. The heavy clomp, clomping resonated as the massive Holstein entered through the barn door. The goosebumps subsided, and a sense of comfort washed over me from knowing that Pa was close, although unaware of my presence just a few feet away. I smiled at the one-sided conversation between Pa and the oblivious cow. "Whoa, easy there. Come on, come on. Hold it, easy, easy. Move it, move it. Okay, stop, stop. That's it, good." Not a single word would be understood by the cow, but farmers always said them, just in case. If you've never lived on a farm or witnessed a cow guided into a stanchion, you'd be surprised by the coaxing and cajoling required to get even a minimal amount of cooperation.

Soon, Pa's random phrases transitioned into the rhythmic sound of milk streams hitting the steel bottom of the milking pail. The milking continued for several minutes, occasionally accompanied by a few more soothing phrases from Pa: "Easy, boss, easy, boss. That's it, nice and easy."

Throughout the milking session, I sensed a somber and sorrowful mood emanating from Pa. He didn't sing his usual hymns, but it was no wonder—his son was missing, possibly having run away from home.

Then, the milking concluded. The sound of squirting milk was replaced by the awkward noises of the cow backing out of the stanchion and clomping out of the barn. Darkness engulfed the surroundings as Pa left through the side door, taking the comforting bits of lantern light with him.

I couldn't bear the underworld darkness of my hideout any longer. Fear and foreboding gnawed at my courage and rationality. Slowly, I emerged from beneath the barn, maintaining a safe distance as I cautiously followed the lantern light across the field toward the house.

As soon as Pa entered the house with the lantern and the pail of milk, I slipped into the woodshed to collect my thoughts. I needed a few moments to prepare myself for the inevitable emotional outpouring. In my mind, I envisioned a grief-stricken family, too distraught to even search for me. They likely assumed I had vanished, perhaps traveling miles away. By now, in their minds, I could be riding a freight train or hitchhiking to another state.

When I felt adequately composed, I left the woodshed and stood at the back door of the house. "Here goes," I whispered to myself. Straightening my shoulders, I stepped through the door and into the kitchen.

Silence enveloped the house. Pa placed large Mason jars filled with milk into the icebox. Ma sat at the far end of the kitchen table, meticulously stitching a patch onto a pair of blue denim pants. Bits played with a doll on the floor beneath the table. Ma briefly glanced in my direction but continued her mending. I walked over to the living room doorway and surveyed the room. Annie Oakley occupied one end of the davenport, reading a magazine. Mutt sat at the other end, repeating a Bible memory verse to herself. Batis arranged a circle of chicken feathers on the floor, Dez spun round and round on the swivel stool at the pump organ. I could hear the muffled conversation between Dave and Odin from their bedroom upstairs. Taking a few steps into the room, I cleared my throat, but no one looked my way.

I wanted to say something, but my mind drew a blank. I turned and walked back into the kitchen, where all remained quiet. I won't say anything, I resolved within myself. Not until someone asked me about my departure.

"What were you doing under the barn all day?" Ma finally broke the silence, her words exploding in my head, swirling around and crashing into a chaotic pile of debris. Devastated and speechless, I stood there in shock. Ma continued her mending, seemingly unaffected, which gave me a moment to gather my shattered thoughts. A long period of silence ensued, and slowly, a few coherent ideas began to form in my damaged cranium. I was about to mention studying the history of the large stumps beneath the barn when Ma added, "And why do you have oatmeal stuck to your eyebrow and in your ear?"

For that, I had no answer. I stood there looking foolish, fully aware of my colossal failure. In a daze, I started stumbling toward the stairs, seeking refuge from the devastating interrogation. Just then, Annie Oakley brushed past me. She paused briefly, leaned over, and whispered into my oatmeal-spattered ear, "Sounds like an UNAUTHORIZED DEPARTURE to me."

Her nickname, Anne Oakly fooled no one. Priscilla could not ride a horse, nor could she shoot a gun. Priscilla's claim of royal blood allowed her to rise above her backwoods roots.

As the eldest of eight siblings, Odin and Dave claimed special
status within the family. Thus, neither acquired a nickname.

Dave at sixteen, dressed in his Sunday best,
poses with his 1936 Chevy Sedan.

CHAPTER 13

——— •⋅• ———

EARLY BUS

I t was midafternoon, and the second-floor classroom of Roosevelt School was oppressively hot and stuffy. The row of hot water radiators against one wall emitted mournful groans and popping sounds, contributing to the stifling atmosphere that hindered any learning. Most of my classmates were either half asleep or gazing blankly out the windows, but I remained alert and fixated on the large clock above the door. Despite my fellow students' drowsiness, Mrs. Fraser, my fourth-grade teacher, persistently droned on, scratching the blackboard with a fresh stick of chalk.

While Mrs. Fraser continued her wearisome lecture, my attention was fixed on the space above the door, as I eagerly awaited the final seconds of this torturous day. As the clock neared twenty minutes to three, I hastily stuffed my books and a few blank sheets of notebook paper into my desk and made a beeline for the door.

Startled that someone was awake, let alone attempting to escape, Mrs. Fraser spun around from the blackboard. In her haste, the stick of chalk snapped in two and shot across the hardwood floor in my direction.

"And just where do you think you're going, young man?" she barked, prompting snickers to ripple through the room. I picked up the chalk from the floor, placed it in her outstretched hand, and repeated the words I had uttered on numerous occasions before:

"EARLY BUS," I enunciated slowly, carefully emphasizing each word. The class erupted into laughter, but their amusement was short-lived. Mrs. Fraser turned her attention back to the class, all the while maintaining a vise-like grip on my bony shoulder.

"There are twenty more minutes of study. Any more laughter, and the rest of you will be writing penalty papers," she scolded.

"Dismissed," she grumbled, flinging me toward the door. I quickly regained my composure after the headlong lurch, allowing me to open the door and escape into the hallway.

I paused for a moment, looking back into the room, while brushing chalky fingerprints off my shirt. Some of the kids wore stone-faced expressions, looking straight ahead, while others struggled to suppress forbidden laughter. Mrs. Vise Fingers slammed the door behind me, but her yelling could still be heard as I skipped down the hall to catch Early Bus.

Early Bus was the only aspect of the Arlington School District that aligned with my educational philosophy. While most students toiled in class until three o'clock, the two dozen kids who lived on and around Burn Hill were released twenty minutes early every day. This unique arrangement resulted from the school district's inability to afford an additional bus solely for the Burn Hill gang. Instead, one bus serviced two routes. After dropping off the Burn Hill students, the bus driver would return to the school around twenty minutes past three to transport the unfortunate souls who rode the "late bus."

My early departure from Mrs. Fraser's class was well known and expected by my hapless classmates, as they recognized that their own freedom was a mere twenty minutes away. However, my untimely exit often caught Mrs. Fraser off guard, necessitating yet another explanation for my early departure.

While my time imprisoned in the classroom rarely sparked my interest, the ride on Early Bus was an entirely different story. The Burn Hill route had long been a challenging one for drivers, as the passengers considered themselves masters of everything but steering the bus. Any new driver quickly learned that even steering was a privilege that could be revoked at any moment.

Even before I became a passenger, I was aware that Early Bus was akin to a voyage on troubled seas, with the possibility of mutiny accompanying each trip. In the rare event that a driver managed to gain control over the rowdy Burn Hill riders, they faced the daunting prospect of dealing with irate parents, ensuring that the driver understood Burn Hill protocol.

There was a particular incident involving Skip Melum, who was kicked off the bus for what the driver called "behavior detrimental to the safety and welfare of others." Skip was informed that he could no longer ride the bus and needed to find an alternative means of transportation. Yet, the following morning, Skip and others waited by the roadside as usual. The others included a few of the Hale kids, since the farm where Skip lived was right next door. When the driver stopped the bus and opened the door, Skip stood first in line ready to board.

The driver left his seat and positioned himself in the doorway, "So you think you can defy my orders and board this bus, do you?"

Just then, a menacing figure emerged from the group outside the bus. This imposing figure wore rugged bib overalls, tall hobnail boots, and a hard hat. Pushing through the waiting students, he grasped the doorframe with his rough, gnarled hand and stepped onto the bus. The bus driver found himself face-to-face with Mr. Norman Melum, Skip's steel-eyed and unshaven father. Mr. Melum, accustomed to dealing with rough men in his logging work, wasted no time on pleasantries and pressed his unshaven face close to the flustered driver's.

Mr. Melum was a man who dealt with situations without regard to feelings, social code, or formalities. As a logger, he spent long, hard days working alongside the roughest, meanest, and orneriest men in the county. He worked in the woods, battling brushy, steep mountain sides and wrestling giant timber and choker cables. He would not be stepping off this bus until there was a clear understanding on the part of this soft and flabby bus jockey that his boy would be, "Riding the bus this day and every day in the future." Skip sat with his friends as usual in the back of the bus.

I vividly remember my first day on Early Bus. Gripped by a sense of foreboding, I chose a seat near the front, anticipating some impending disaster. I had heard countless stories of fights and confrontations with drivers, leaving me petrified as I prepared for the worst. Surprisingly, nothing alarming occurred on that initial day, but I quickly discerned which students were most likely to engage in future chaos.

Brothers Carl and Gene Zaretzke, as well as Alex Sancrant, swaggered onto the bus with an air of arrogance, while Junior Luthi, whom I suspected to be a catalyst for unrest, exuded a rebellious aura. These older boys, along with a few younger kids and even some girls, displayed a distinct disdain for authority and the rules of ridership. Most days, I sat with my good friend Bob Hoy, and due to our parents' close friendship and communication, we made a conscious effort not to create any disturbances that might find their way back to them.

The Burn Hill bus route wound its way along a narrow road in a dark, densely forested canyon. On the right side, a steep embankment led down to a creek, where moss-covered boulders stood amidst tall ferns, spiny devil's club, and patches of nettles, all beneath a canopy of towering maple trees. For Bus Number 8, the journey up Burn Hill proved to be an arduous task, draining the bus's horsepower as it labored to transport the Early Bus gang to their respective homes five days a week.

Most bus drivers assigned to the Early Bus route had short tenures. The demanding nature of the route, coupled with constant challenges from the unruly riders, prompted many drivers to seek alternative employment. One driver stands out in my memory: a gray-haired, middle-aged man named Wes, who possessed a soft and timid demeanor that seemed ill-suited for driving Early Bus.

While the frazzled bus driver focused his limited abilities on the challenge of Burn Hill, the old bus complemented the scene with its own limitations. The rubber-tired conveyor of student cargo could scarcely be considered much of an improvement over a yellow-painted prairie schooner. Bus Number 8 was grossly underpowered for the challenge of Burn Hill and would often be overheated and steaming as it neared the top of the mile-long hill.

During one incident, as the bus approached the summit of Burn Hill, it sputtered to a halt. The bus emitted hissing sounds resembling the release of air from thousands of balloons. Steam billowed from the front, obscuring the windshield and momentarily silencing the typically rowdy students.

Driver Wes rose from his seat and faced his attentive audience. "We need water," he declared, motioning toward the creek hidden from view down the steep embankment, tangled in dense vegetation.

Mockingly, a voice from the back of the bus responded, "Yes, we need water."

"I need a big, strong boy to volunteer to fetch some water from the creek," Wes appealed.

No one budged. Even with the emphasis on "a big, strong boy," none of the tough guys stepped forward. Sensing the futility of his request, Wes attempted to reason with them.

"You know, if we don't get some water for this bus, all of you will be late getting home," he implored.

"Why don't you get the water yourself?" came a sarcastic retort from the back.

Wes opened the bus door and peered down the steep embankment. Although the sound of flowing water was audible, the creek bottom was riddled with nettles and devil's club, plants notorious for causing pain and discomfort. Every child on the bus had experienced the torment inflicted by these malicious plants, rendering them unwilling to venture into the creek's depths.

Wes continued to plead for a volunteer but received only unsympathetic responses. After a while, he shrugged his shoulders and left the bus. In a storage bay on the side, he discovered a galvanized pail, which he carried as he stumbled and slid down the embankment, disappearing into the thicket of vegetation. Several minutes passed as the passengers, some peering through windows and others standing outside the bus, watched the scratched and exhausted bus driver struggle back up to the roadside. Sweating profusely, he appeared on the verge of collapse. Wes rested for a few minutes before refilling the bus's radiator.

As the bus restarted and resumed its journey, a touch of sympathy seemed to wash over the passengers. This wave of compassion even reached the tough guys at the back. Upon Junior Luthi's exit at the next stop, he patted Wes on the shoulder and offered a rare compliment, "You did okay today. We may even recommend you for a raise in pay."

Such words were as close to praise as one could hope for as an early bus driver. However, any sympathy for the tormented driver was short-lived, as the unruly riders quickly reclaimed their dominance. A fight broke out on the bus one day, involving two boys who wrestled and crashed over seats and down the aisle, occupying a significant portion of the bus. Frightened students scrambled to the front, attempting to avoid becoming collateral damage. Boys yelled and girls screamed while Wes did his best to navigate the winding canyon road.

With no safe shoulder to pull the bus to the side, the bus driver, increasingly agitated and distracted, was compelled to keep driving until finding a suitable spot. Meanwhile, the bus swayed from side to side as passengers shifted back and forth, striving to distance themselves from the chaos.

Finally, outside the canyon, Wes found a place to safely park the bus. The fight continued as he stood up to address the agitated crowd. It took several attempts, but Wes eventually managed to calm the frenzied students and separate the exhausted combatants. Tears filled his eyes as he weakly and tremblingly tried to restore order.

After everyone returned to their seats, except for the two pugilists standing in the aisle beside Wes, a fragile semblance of calm settled over the bus. We listened in anticipation, wondering what punishment would be meted out to the troublemakers.

"You two have caused a terrible situation on this bus," Wes quivered, his lower lip quivering. "You will have to leave the bus immediately and walk home."

The Supreme Court of the bus then intervened. Carl, Gene, Junior, and Alex, the influential boys at the back of the bus, rose and delivered their verdict, speaking on behalf of their self-appointed court.

"No one is leaving this bus."

The ruling was final and uncontestable, leaving Wes no choice but to return to his seat and resume his duties, driving Early Bus students to their destinations. Order had been restored, but not in the manner Wes would have preferred.

However, there was at least one instance when the Supreme Court of Early Bus did not intervene. This may have been because half the members of the court had already exited the bus two stops before. On this occasion the bus driver's judgment prevailed. There was a fist fight between Roy Sundquist and me. The altercation was short-lived, resulting in Roy with a bloody nose. Witnessing the blood, Roy began screaming as if he was bleeding to death. His hysterics caught Wes's attention, leading him to believe a tragedy was imminent. The bus screeched to a halt, and Roy, blubbering and bleeding, found himself at the front of the bus, staining the horrified driver with his blood.

Roy collapsed onto the bus floor, his eyes darting erratically. He blurted out incomprehensible words, as though attempting to utter his final farewell. Witnessing the distressing scene, Wes himself grew queasy and weak-kneed, appearing pale and helpless as he searched for assistance. Soon, Roy's sister, Lois, arrived by his side. She helped Roy sit up and tilted his head back, managing to calm him down and halt the bleeding.

Wes surveyed the remaining children on the bus. With a weak and trembling voice, he inquired, "Who did this?"

A dozen fingers pointed at me. Wes escorted me to the front of the bus and ordered me off. I stepped out onto the roadside and watched as a chorus of hands waved at me from the windows. As the bus roared away, its exhaust pipe kicked up a cloud of dust that engulfed me. Not a very pleasant farewell, I thought to myself. Blinking and rubbing my dust-filled eyes, I oriented myself and realized I stood just across the ditch from a barbed wire fence that marked the boundary of our farm's lower field. On the other side of the fence, a four-legged creature wagged its tail. I hopped the fence, and Queenie, our loyal dog, accompanied me as I walked through the field toward home.

If I were to claim that everyone on Early Bus was rowdy, insensitive, or a troublemaker, I would be overlooking a few well-behaved and gentle souls. Among them was Ginger, a quiet girl who occupied a seat near the front. Not only was Ginger reserved and polite, but she also possessed an undeniable charm. With her long, dark curls cascading around her shoulders, green eyes, cute dimples, and a charming sway in her walk, Ginger epitomized the image of a lovely school bus passenger. In truth, she couldn't be classified as a typical Burn Hill kid since she resided in the peaceful valley at the base of Burn Hill. Ginger led a tranquil life with her parents, older sister, and younger brother on a serene dairy farm nestled in a hidden valley along the Stillaguamish River's south fork. Unlike the Hale household, Ginger's home exuded tranquility, moderation, and sensibility. To any driver of Early Bus, Ginger was the ideal passenger—quiet and polite, uninvolved in the anarchy that often plagued the bus. Seated on the right side, Ginger enjoyed views of the tumbling creek in the canyon, wisely choosing to ignore the surrounding chaos.

Little did I know that this adorable girl would eventually become my wife. Perhaps if I had recognized this fate, I would have spent less time acting foolishly at the back of the bus and more time engaging in meaningful conversations with her at the front, discussing the beauty of the creek.

Wes eventually retired from his position as the Early Bus driver. Rumor had it that he left Arlington, seeking employment in a more civilized community. In 1958, when I was twelve years old, the Hale family bid farewell to Arlington and Burn Hill.

Years later, during my attendance at a large city high school, I once again found myself riding a bus to and from school. The luxury of getting out twenty minutes early was forever gone. The fascinating phenomenon of Early Bus had become nothing more than a cherished memory. However, I would have one last encounter with Wes, the tormented bus driver.

One day after school, as I walked past a long row of parked buses, I glanced into an open bus door and made a surprising discovery. I stepped back, stunned and disbelieving. I stood in front of the open door, and the driver inside peered out, his expression one of nervous confusion. Squirming in his seat, he struggled to find words, desperately trying to place my tall, skinny frame and face in context. I watched for a while as he wrestled with memories he had long sought to bury. Sensing that he had endured enough torment, I moved closer to the open door and looked directly into his fearful eyes.

Leaning forward, I quietly mouthed the two words he had hoped to never hear again. "Early Bus," I whispered.

Andrew, Marilyn, Reuben, Priscilla. Ma never allowed for even a hint of poverty when she prepared her kids for school.

CHAPTER 14

————— •+• —————

THE ART OF TRACTORING

"I'm going outside to move the tractor out of the rain," I declared, mustering as much manliness as nine-year-old could.

Ma didn't lift her gaze from the ironing. "The rain has stopped," she replied. "Besides, your Pa needs the tractor when he gets home. He plans to cut wood this afternoon and will require the tractor for the buzzsaw. Why don't you leave it where it is?"

Of course, Ma knew my true intentions were to drive the big red Farmall. At nine years old, I had become quite skilled at coming up with impromptu justifications. "Well," I began, "last time it rained, the magneto-thing on the motor—the one that zaps the spark plugs—got wet, and the tractor wouldn't start."

I had no real understanding of the inner workings of a tractor, but I vaguely remembered Pa mentioning something about a wet magneto. It was at that moment Ma looked up from her ironing and peered at me. I had often experienced this kind of scrutiny, and I recognized it as an assessment of my knowledge regarding electro-mechanical devices. Seeing that Ma probably knew nothing about magnetos, I stood there, pretending to be a concerned mechanic.

"Well, alright, go ahead," she finally acquiesced. I took it as confirmation that Ma was indeed unaware of magnetos, sparks, and tractor-related matters. With that, I quickly put on my boots and rushed out the back door.

If Ma had any concerns about my ability to operate a tractor, she kept them to herself. I had embarked on my first solo tractor ride when I was only seven years old—an age when most boys were still drooling over tractors in the pages of coloring books. Now, at nine years old, I considered myself a seasoned tractor driver.

Farm boys fantasize about tractors long before they even stop breastfeeding, and their first ride often occurs while still in diapers. It seems that fathers derive some sort of manly euphoria from whisking their fragile male infants out of their cribs for a joy ride on a tractor. The belching black smoke from a tractor's exhaust stack becomes the inoculation that prevents a boy from ever enjoying the indoors again. Child psychologists have observed that once a male infant experiences his first tractor ride, any desire to fold laundry is forever eradicated.

Once outside, I meticulously prepared the tractor for starting. As I carried out my tasks, I happily hummed, "Old MacDonald had a farm, e-i-e-i-o." I had carefully learned each step in the process from observing Pa and my older brothers. There was already a chunk of firewood wedged under one of the massive rear tires to prevent the tractor from rolling down the slight incline where it was parked. Climbing onto the seat, I jerked the shift rod into neutral, causing the tractor to lurch forward ever so slightly as the large, knobby tire settled against the piece of firewood.

Stepping off the tractor, I stood there, gazing up at the magnificent machine. I couldn't help but admire the most powerful four-wheeled creature ever to roam Burn Hill. Dave and Odin had convinced me of its extraordinary capabilities, making bold claims about the pulling power of our Farmall F-12. They often scoffed at the more modern and versatile Fordson tractors owned by most farmers. They referred to those smaller machines as "puddle jumpers," insisting they were no match for the F-12, and according to Dave, "couldn't pull the hat off your head."

Dave and Odin had every reason to be proud of our old tractor, for it belonged solely to my older brothers. It had taken them a couple of years of diligent saving to scrape together the money for its purchase—an impressive $500, a considerable sum in 1952. My brothers took great pride in their tractor. Despite being built in 1938, making it 14 years old at the time of their acquisition, the tractor received their utmost affection. It might have been the only Farmall in existence that underwent regular washes and even the occasional waxing. They even adorned the radiator cap of the old Farmall with a flying lady hood ornament. This elegantly chromed lady with wings was the same graceful figure that once graced the hood of Pa's 1932 Plymouth sedan. In those days, these sleek ornaments lent an air of speed and allure to otherwise ordinary cars, and so many unassuming automobiles, including a 1932 Plymouth, were equipped with them.

Dave and Odin had also affixed two gaudy, four-inch chrome stars to what could be deemed the tractor's dashboard. These were acquired from the popular JC Whitney catalog, a supplier of inexpensive and often tacky automobile accessories. While the old Farmall could be spiffed up like a pampered Cadillac, it could also be seen covered in thick mud and reeking of putrid manure as it dutifully tackled the field and farm work.

A few raindrops splattered against my face, snapping me back to the present task. The challenge before me was not merely driving the large Farmall but igniting its massive engine. I located the choke control ring on the side of the motor, inserted my finger, and pulled. That was the easy part. Standing in front of the tractor, I contemplated the steel crank handle jutting out from the machine. Over the years, many calloused hands had polished the handle to a shine, much like the elegant chrome lady adorning the top of the Farmall. "Alright," I whispered, as if that simple utterance would aid me in the upcoming task.

My method of starting the engine at the age of nine was a testament to mental resilience and applied physics. I had developed a technique known as "gut cranking." I rotated the crank handle until it found a notch around the one o'clock position. With the handle firmly engaged in the beast's heart, I positioned myself beside it and took a deep breath.

Grasping the handle with both hands, I leaped up and onto it, pressing my gut tightly against the crank. The crank grudgingly rotated clockwise to approximately the 5 o'clock position before forcefully kicking back, launching me counterclockwise to around 9 o'clock, where I unceremoniously landed on the ground. The red beast stood defiantly silent.

I wiped the mud from my hands and made another attempt. The tractor needed time to warm up to the idea—this much I knew. Respecting its stubborn nature, I readjusted the handle for another gut-cranking endeavor. I repeated the same counterclockwise trajectory, hitting the ground with each try. The Farmall regarded me with utter disdain. Again and again, I followed the same routine, enduring the same agonizing results. The tractor refused to start.

It is said that one sign of insanity is repeating the same action over and over while expecting different outcomes. At nine years old, I had not yet to come across this piece of wisdom, so I stubbornly persisted, hoping for a different result. My aching gut felt as though it might burst. I experimented with less choke, then more choke, but the beast remained stubbornly dormant.

Exhausted and overwhelmed by pain, I sought refuge in the woodshed. There, I conducted a thorough self-examination, removing my jacket and lifting my shirt to assess my aching abdomen. The area was red with streaks of purple, and I felt the urge to vomit. However, my concern shifted to my ribs, which felt as if they had been crushed. Carefully counting them, I discovered twelve on the right side and only eleven on the left. While the pain made a recount unbearable, I couldn't help but wonder if the asymmetry of my body was further evidence of the accuracy of the biblical account, given that one rib from Adam had been used to create Eve. Leaning against a stack of firewood, I rested my battered body, listening to the rhythmic patter of rain on the shingled roof.

The prospect of death seemed agonizingly slow, so I summoned the strength to venture outside once more for another attempt at gut cranking. I was aware of the dangers associated with the kickback of a tractor's crank, as Pa had regaled me with stories of grown men who had broken their arms in such mishaps. Despite this knowledge, I was determined to try again.

To protect my gut and ribs from further harm, I folded my jacket and placed it over the crank—an ingenious idea, albeit a belated one. My midsection throbbed with pain, and my leap onto the crank handle was feeble. Wincing with each movement, I rode the crank as it descended, half-expecting to be flung backward like wet laundry. But while clutching my jacket against my tormented body, a powerful bang erupted, accompanied by a plume of thick black smoke billowing into the rain-filled sky. The Farmall had come to life and was raring to go!

Pain has a way of dissipating in the presence of music, and the old Farmall unleashed its own rendition of "E-i-e-i-o."

"We're going tractoring!" I exclaimed as I mounted the pulsating beast.

Using my coat to wipe off the rain-soaked seat, I noticed that it was made of steel and painted the same vibrant red as the rest of the tractor. The seat's design was perfectly contoured to accommodate even the most ample posteriors. Several coin-sized holes punctured the seat, whether for ventilation purposes or to allow rainwater drainage remained unclear. Before the advent of cushions, all tractors were built this way.

Many farmers develop a condition colloquially known as "tractor butt," characterized by a considerable widening of their posterior. The scientific community more respectfully labels this posterior ailment "Buttock Gigantuous," attributing it to the countless hours spent perched atop these rough-riding contraptions. It's worth noting that some farmers' wives also experience this condition, though it is unrelated to tractoring.

Positioning my meager backside on the edge of the seat, I stretched my left foot to depress the clutch pedal. The Farmall boasted four forward gears, with the fourth offering only a marginal increase in speed compared to the first. It was a design flaw I would have rectified had I been the engineer behind the Farmall F-12. The throttle, situated next to the steering wheel, required no adjustment for this adventure, as it was already set for maximum enjoyment. With the release of the clutch, the boy and the tractor entered into an intimate partnership.

It seemed a shame to simply drive the Farmall to its shelter—a dug-out area beneath the house resembling an enlarged root cellar, primarily used for storing potatoes and burying carrots in a cold, damp sand pit. While my ultimate plan was to park the tractor in that space, there was a compelling reason to indulge in some tractoring beforehand. Yes, it was raining, but after the torturous ordeal of the past hour, it seemed fitting to reward myself with an extended drive.

The plan materialized in an instant. There was no internal debate or wisdom whispering in my ear. I steered the Farmall up through the orchard, purposely avoiding the view of the house's windows. I didn't want Ma to discover that I had no intention of moving the tractor to its designated storage location. Nor did I wish to entertain the possibility of my thoughts being telepathically transmitted through the orchard and into Ma's mind—I had witnessed her doing just that on other occasions. To divert any unwanted mental interference, I continued to hum "Old MacDonald Had a Farm," hoping that innocent brain waves would prevail.

The town was three miles away, mostly downhill, but my goal wasn't to reach that far. I merely aimed to descend the long hill to gauge the Farmall's maximum speed. This would be an experience foreign to the old tractor, as my plan involved shifting into neutral and letting the formidable laws of gravity take over.

I had dabbled in freewheeling with the tractor once before on the wooded hill behind the barn. A rudimentary logging road spiraled down through the trees from the hilltop to the flat land below. Badis and Des clung to the back of the tractor like leeches to a hog as we embarked on that exhilarating descent. We emerged relatively unscathed, save for an encounter with a leaning alder tree that loomed over the outer curve of the road. It was then that the conspicuous red can-like object on the side of the motor was dislodged. Later, I discovered it was not a mere red can but a somewhat essential component of the motor. Pa was surprised it had broken off for no apparent reason. Dave lamented the resulting scratches and small dent, while Odin fumed over my failure to promptly park the tractor after the incident. He argued that driving through dirt and dust without an air-filtering system could have irreversibly damaged the motor.

All I could muster in response was, "I thought it was just a red can thing."

To which Odin retorted, "That's what you get for thinking when you're not accustomed to it."

Continuing my rendition of "Old MacDonald Had a Farm," I left the driveway. It felt like passing through a portal into a new realm. Glancing back through the frame of mock orange bushes that flanked the entrance, I could see the entire length of the gravel driveway, stretching all the way to the house. Ma was nowhere in sight. The melody of "Old MacDonald" resounded in my mind, infusing new life and meaning into the familiar tune: "All is clear on the farm, e-i-e-i-oooooo …" With the tractor shifted into neutral, we were freewheeling and accelerating down Burn Road. The pavement was slick and wet, water spraying off the back of the fat knobby tires and shooting skyward. The old tractor came alive, exceeding my wildest expectations. The flying lady hood ornament seemed poised for flight, her wings outstretched. Rain pelted my face, obscuring my vision. The thunderous roar of the tires drowned out the engine's sound. Still, there was no sage voice of wisdom perched upon my shoulder. "E-i-e-i-o!" I bellowed amid the tire's cacophony and the drenching spray.

Steering proved surprisingly ineffectual, as if the Farmall possessed a will of its own, darting down the road with an unsettling wobble reminiscent of a three-legged hippopotamus wearing a rocket pack. I did my best to keep the tractor centered on the road, while the woods on either side blurred into a haze of shadows. Meeting an uphill-bound car seemed unlikely, but I was willing to take my chances. The old Farmall reveled in speed but had no concept of maintaining a straight path.

I would only apply the brakes if things got worse, which they immediately did. I lost control of the wobbling tractor, which began bouncing and violently jerking from side to side. One moment, I was veering towards the right ditch; the next, it was the left ditch. The big, wobbly tires on either side of me blurred into a disorienting frenzy. Although I tried to focus on the road ahead, the terrifying sight of the tires made concentration impossible. I found myself engulfed in a world of terror—a whirlwind of wobbling black masses shrouded in spray. Gripping the steering wheel as tightly as possible served no real purpose other than to prevent me from being thrown into one of those swirling black blobs. The tires, which I had always assumed were made of hard rubber, now appeared as contorted masses flopping and wobbling like whale blubber. It was in that moment that the little wisdom guy on my shoulder finally made his presence felt. He didn't utter a word, for he was just trying to hold on. Even with my limited intelligence, I realized that I should apply the brakes, but that was easier said than done.

The brakes on a 1938 Farmall F-12 consist of two tall hand levers, one on each side of the cockpit. Each lever controlled one rear brake—one lever for the right brake, the other for the left. I didn't need the little wisdom guy to know that my wobbling rocket was in serious trouble. But to work the brakes, I would have to let go of the steering wheel, and I needed both hands for that. The little wisdom guy was still holding on, but he couldn't offer any suggestions. It seemed inevitable—I was going to die.

I had considered the situation long before it came into view. Just ahead, where a creek crossed under the road, there was a fork in the road. If I had any chance of survival, I would have to make a right turn. After the turn, the road would level out. I doubted I would be alive to make the right turn, but just in case, I fought to stay on the road. My skinny backside was wedged against the edge of the seat, and my feet braced against any footholds they could find. With each passing moment, I was losing control as we hurtled towards the treacherous turn at the creek. Visibility was poor; I could barely see. I had been struggling to maintain some semblance of vision through the spray, but now the road ahead was nothing but a watery blur. Occasionally, I caught glimpses that allowed me to attempt steering adjustments. The critical right turn was approaching.

The next few seconds were a whirlwind of confusion. Time seemed to slow down. My body tensed with fear, and the chaos overwhelmed any capacity for thought or reaction. If my presence on the tractor offered any assistance in surviving, it was purely accidental. I felt the lateral g-forces and desperately fought to avoid being thrown from the tractor. Whether the tractor was successfully navigating the turn, I couldn't determine. All I could do was cling tightly to the steering wheel and try to keep my scrawny backside connected to the seat.

And then, the tractor began to slow down. I struggled to regain some semblance of vision. The wobbling tires gradually stabilized, and the deafening sound of throbbing rubber subsided. Things were definitely slowing down, and the steering wheel started to respond to my trembling hands. It all felt surreal, as I tried to separate reality from fear. Eventually, the old Farmall rolled to an ever-so-gentle stop.

It was then that I reached for one of the levers and instinctively applied some brake. The brakes weren't necessary, but it was an automatic response from my terrified body. My arms fell limply to my sides as I blinked away the water that had flooded my eyes. My ears were ringing. The motor sounded strangely quiet, as if I were hearing it from a great distance. After several minutes of stunned confusion, I began to survey my surroundings. Miraculously, I was sitting on a level stretch of road. I gazed into the dense woods on my right and gradually recognized the stark white trunks of birch trees. I immediately knew where I was; I had helped Pa cut firewood in this very spot. It belonged to Mickie Ryan, who owned the butcher shop and cold storage locker in town. Mickie had granted Pa permission to cut firewood from this area. I was a hundred yards past the treacherous turn.

"Are you okay, Andrew?"

The voice came from my left. That's when I noticed a vehicle stopped right next to me in the road. I didn't recognize the voice, only that it belonged to a raspy, female speaker. I instantly recognized the oxidized red panel truck—it belonged to Mrs. Sundquist, a neighbor who lived just half a mile up the hill from our farm. She gawked at me with her head halfway out of the side window, a cigarette wobbling at the corner of her mouth. The smoke escaping through the open window mingled with the damp air.

"Are you okay?" she asked again.

Well, yes, I guessed I was okay, but hadn't had time to come to that conclusion. Mrs. Sunquist would know nothing about my wild ride, since she was coming from the direction of town.

"Yup, I'm okay," I managed to mumble. "Just looking at the white birch trees."

I realized my response was foolish, but my mind was still caught up in the moment, somewhere back at the treacherous turn in the road. I tried to calm myself. Mrs. Sundquist took a long drag on her cigarette, studying me intently. Slowly, she exhaled, and long, lazy ribbons of smoke curled through her hair.

"Yup, I'm fine," I muttered before she could ask again.

I had no strength left. My trembling body was on the verge of toppling off the tractor, while my mind struggled to convince it to stay put. I weakly waved a hand towards the woods. "White birch trees," I mumbled, though it probably sounded incoherent and disconnected from the present reality. The smoke lady continued to stare at me.

"White birch trees," I repeated for no apparent reason, other than feeling the need to speak. I despised this kind of interrogation, especially when I was trying to recover from my near-death experience.

"Cold out here, isn't it?" she finally said.

"Not really. Well, maybe a little ... I'm heading home now."

"Good idea. You should get a raincoat. You'll catch a cold."

And with that, the smoke lady vanished. A hazy blue cloud of smoke lingered in the air above the road.

I was cold. I turned the tractor around and began making my way home. The tractor purred along smoothly, as if nothing had happened. As I rounded the treacherous turn, I scanned the area, half expecting to find tractor parts scattered about. But there was nothing—only a faint oil sheen on the pavement, shimmering in iridescent rainbow colors.

By the time I reached my driveway, my nerves had settled. I hadn't been gone for long. The mile-long dash to the birch trees had likely set a world speed record for a tractor. I skillfully maneuvered the old Farmall into the safety of the driveway and parked it near the buzzsaw. There was no need to shelter it now since Pa would be returning home soon. I made a quick stop at the outhouse before entering the kitchen through the back door.

"You're soaking wet," Ma remarked as she continued ironing.

I needed dry clothes, so I hastily made my way up the stairs to my bedroom. Halfway up, I heard Ma calling after me, "Did you have a good drive?" I pretended not to hear and lay on my bed for a while, replaying the ill-conceived tractor ride in my mind.

I was still upstairs when I heard the tractor start. Peering out my bedroom window, I saw Pa moving the Farmall. Dave and Odin were with him. The three of them had just returned from town. How close was that? I had narrowly missed crossing paths with them on the road by mere minutes. What if ...? I pushed the thought aside. I didn't want to dwell on it. I didn't stay in the house for further questioning. As I passed through the kitchen, my haughty sister scrutinized me, as if she wanted to say something. I didn't give her the chance. In a flash, I was back outside.

Pa was preparing the tractor for the buzzsaw. He had shut down the tractor and was extending the fifteen-foot-long belt between the buzzsaw pulley and the tractor pulley. The buzzsaw, mounted on skids, was an imposing piece of equipment. With its three-foot circular saw blade and sharp, jagged teeth, it could swiftly cut through logs. However, it was notorious not only for being an efficient firewood cutting machine but also for its potential to cause serious injuries, including severed fingers, hands, and limbs.

As Pa set up the equipment, my mind was still preoccupied with the death-defying descent down Burn Hill. I couldn't comprehend why the Farmall had become so uncontrollable on the downhill run. While Pa was busy getting ready to start the tractor, I saw an opportunity to engage him in a conversation that would provide the answers I sought without confessing my own involvement.

"How fast can this tractor go?" I asked innocently.

Pa looked at me, seemingly surprised by the question. "Not fast at all," he replied. "These old tractors were never built for speed; they were designed for work."

His response sounded reasonable, but I was still curious about why the tractor had bounced and the tires had wobbled. So, I made another attempt to get the information I wanted.

"But what if you put it in neutral and went downhill?"

Pa glanced at me, as if to convey that no one would be foolish enough to attempt such a thing. He didn't provide an answer, but Dave chimed in with his perspective.

"Let me tell you something," Dave interjected, "these old tractors were never built for speed—"

I interrupted him, finishing his sentence, "They were built for work."

"It's not a joke," Dave snapped. "I'm serious. These old tractors can't handle high speeds. If you try to go downhill in neutral, you'll end up getting yourself killed, no doubt about it."

"Why?" I inquired, genuinely curious.

"Because the rear tires are filled with 75 percent liquid calcium chloride and a little air on top. When you pick up too much speed, the liquid becomes unbalanced inside the tires. That's when the tractor starts wobbling and shaking uncontrollably. You won't be able to steer. You will crash and die."

Dave stared at me intensely, making sure his message sank in. "You understand?" he asked sternly.

"Wow!" I exclaimed. "How do you know all this stuff?"

Odin pointed to one of the rear tires and demonstrated. He pulled out a folding knife, opened the blade, and knelt beside the tire. He poked the center of the valve stem, and a milky white liquid squirted out.

"See?" he said.

"Wow!" I repeated, amazed. "How did you learn that the liquid causes the tires to go crazy?"

"It's basic knowledge," Odin explained. "It's about scientific principles like centrifugal rotation, momentum, and inertia. All of that is going on inside those big tires. Most people don't think about it."

"That's for sure," I muttered to myself.

Odin continued pouring technical jargon into my mind, but Pa moved to the front of the tractor, signaling his intention to start the engine. Grasping the crank handle with both hands, he gave it a swift rotation. The tractor roared to life. I instinctively placed my hands on my sore stomach and ribs, longing for the day when my gut cranking would be a distant memory.

The piercing sound of the buzzsaw blade and vivid images of gruesome accidents made me uneasy, so I sought refuge in the safety of the woodshed. From there, I observed the firewood cutting operation.

Later that evening, during supper, Ma mentioned that Mrs. Sundquist had visited earlier in the day. As Ma spoke, her gaze fixed on me, and I was caught off guard. My mouth dropped open, and some bits of carrot fell onto my lap.

"That was nice." The tone of Pa's voice was one of apathy. Not that he was being rude; it was just the kind of response Pa would give when he was deep in thought about something else.

Ma continued staring at me, prompting me to wonder what the smoke lady had said. Did she inform Ma about seeing me on the tractor near Mickie Ryan's property—shaking, scared, and incoherent? Could Mrs. Sundquist have revealed that information?

The subject was dropped, and there was no further discussion about Mrs. Sundquist's visit. Nobody at the table could possibly know about my wild ride, yet uncertainty lingered. Why had the smoke lady stopped by the house? Had she informed Ma? I needed to clarify matters. I had to ask Ma directly what the smoke lady had said. I mustered the courage to speak up.

Before I could voice my question, Ma spoke first. "Mrs. Sundquist mentioned that you were looking at white birch trees. She also seemed concerned that you didn't have a raincoat. The raincoat part makes sense, but white birch trees?"

Ma paused for a few seconds, pondering the situation. Then she continued, "I don't understand what she was talking about. There are no white birch trees around here. In fact, I doubt there's white birch trees within a mile of our place."

"That sounds about right," I replied. "You'd have to go all the way down to Mickie Ryan's woods to find white birch trees."

"But you couldn't have driven the old slow-poke Farmall to Mickie Ryan's and back in the time you were gone," Ma reasoned.

"No way!" I chuckled. "Not unless I let the dynamics of centrifugal rotation and the unbalanced momentum and inertia take control." I had no real idea what I was saying, but it felt good to say it.

Ma smiled at me. "That would be a sight to see," she remarked.

"Yes, it would," I whispered to myself.

The Farmall F-12 willingly agrees for a photo with Andrew, Reuben and Marilyn on top, while Stephen poses in front.

CHAPTER 15

A MAJOR DISCOVERY

I always had a desire to go fishing, but unfortunately, fishing wasn't a common activity in my family. Although Dave and Odin had fishing gear, they rarely used it. I saw this as a family flaw and a lack of responsible stewardship. I was determined to change that. I wanted to go fishing, but I didn't know where to go.

Dave and Odin occasionally mentioned a lake deep in the woods near our Burn Hill home. They called it "Holms Lake." While they knew about it, they refused to share the location with me. I decided to gather information subtly by asking questions.

"Is the lake big, with boats and a swimming area?" I inquired innocently, hoping to learn more about its whereabouts.

"You don't even know how to swim," Odin replied quickly.

"I know, but I'm just wondering if people swim there," I persisted.

"No one swims there because most people don't even know the lake exists. Plus, the water is brown," Odin explained.

"Why is the water brown?" I asked.

"It's brown because it's surrounded by a peat bog," Odin responded.

I had no idea what a peat bog was, but I shook my head in acknowledgment. I would ask Pa about peat bogs later.

"What about boats?" I asked.

"No boat has ever been on that lake, and good luck trying to get a boat in there without dragging it through a big patch of nettles," Odin responded.

Odin was determined not to disclose the location of the lake, and for good reason. As a non-swimmer, I should not be going anywhere near a lake. Despite Odin's attempt to not share information about the lake's location, he'd already unwittingly given me a valuable clue.

I pretended ignorance about the nettles, even though I knew exactly where they were located. The neighboring Melum property had a significant nettle patch near the back of their field. I figured heading in that direction might lead me to the lake.

"Are there nettles near the lake?" I asked, expecting Odin to end the conversation. Surprisingly, he continued.

"Nope, you have to go far beyond the nettles. There's no trail, and it's real brushy, with windfalls and big cedar trees." Odin's single sentence provided a wealth of information. The mention of big cedar trees was particularly helpful since our property had mostly fir and alder trees, while the Melum property had abundant cedar trees.

Before ending our conversation, Odin shared one last intriguing and frightening detail.

"And one more thing: The lake is bottomless," he warned.

I couldn't comprehend the concept of a bottomless lake, but as I struggled to find words, Odin repeated his statement, leaving me both scared and fascinated.

Although my knowledge of the lake and its location was limited, I began making plans for a fishing trip. Mutt and Batis agreed to join me in my search for Holms Lake. We quietly took Dave and Odin's fishing poles and a small box of tackle, keeping our intentions secret. Our destination was Melum's field and the nettle patch.

As we pondered why anyone would drag a boat through nettles, we decided to walk around them. I led the way, assuring Mutt and Batis that I had gathered enough information to find the lake.

The first half mile of our journey followed a familiar route, which didn't necessarily lead to the lake but would take us to the Robison family dump site. Explorers often get sidetracked, and the allure of the dump was too strong to resist. We had no intention of abandoning our mission, but a quick stop at the dump seemed logical.

We had visited the dump site before, where a treasure trove of discarded items awaited. The site belonged not only to the Robisons but also to the Sundquist family. It never occurred to me to ask why the Sundquists dumped their garbage there, but later I learned that Mrs. Sundquist was the daughter of the Robisons.

Excitedly, we rummaged through the debris, searching for toys. Although the elderly Robisons didn't discard toys, the Sundquists' son seemed to dispose of them regularly. Among the trash, we discovered a pedal car with a flattened back end. Despite the damage, the blue and white paint still shimmered, and we optimistically believed we could repair it. We set the pedal car aside, intending to retrieve it later after finding the lake.

While we lost ourselves in the dump, Mutt grew impatient and reminded us of our mission to find the lake.

"How do you expect to find the lake without a map?" Mutt challenged.

I pulled Pa's army surplus compass out of my pocket and set it on a stump. The pointer swung around and pointed in the opposite direction we were traveling. I picked it up, turned it 180 degrees and set it down again. The stubborn pointer seemed determined to point in only one direction, and it was not the way we wanted to travel.

"Something ain't right," I muttered. The compass was either broken or I didn't know how to use it. I determined it was broken.

As we ventured deeper into the wilderness, the idea of discovering a lake became daunting. However, the presence of big cedars, windfalls, and brush was just as Odin had described. I've heard it said, "It's better to be lucky than good." This is a statement that would certainly apply to this trio of unskilled explorers. There was no skill in finding the lake, but find it, we did.

But this was no ordinary lake. It lacked easy access, grassy shores, or sandy beaches. It was about three to four acres in size, surrounded by decaying alder trees, some choking the shoreline, while others stood in the water. Towering above them were giant cedar trees, long dead and limbless, appearing like eerie one-hundred-foot-tall black spires. Fallen trees scattered across the water's surface near the shore, and long-legged water striders skated across the brownish water. A thin layer of misty fog hung low, and the only sound was the occasional distant woodpecker hammering on a rotting alder.

For a while, none of us spoke. The silence of the place demanded it. The ground surrounding the lake was moss-covered and spongy. Every step we took caused us to sink silently until water squished around our feet. Wide-eyed, we stood there, trying to comprehend the surreal scene before us.

Using fallen trees near the shoreline, we attempted to fish, even though we had no fishing expertise. We tried every fishing lure in the repurposed metal box that once held Singer sewing machine attachments. We might have done just as well with sewing machine attachments, for the tackle we used proved depressingly ineffective. Some of the tackle became detached from my line and sunk into the depths. The thought of Odin's claim about the bottomless lake filled my mind with fear.

Then, Batis announced he had found something: a boat.

Unfazed, Mutt and I continued fishing. "There ain't no boats anywhere around here." We both chuckled quietly.

"No, it's a real boat, and you have to see it," Batis insisted.

From where I was standing, I could see a large log with huckleberry bushes growing on it.

"A boat with huckleberries?" we scoffed.

"I'm serious! It's a boat! You have to see it," Batis persisted.

Carefully, I made my way off the log I had been fishing from, still haunted by the notion of a bottomless lake. I crossed the squishy moss to join Batis, who pointed at the shore.

There it was—a blackened hulk of a watercraft. The back half was submerged in water, while the front half rested on the shore, partially sunken in the moss.

"It's an Indian dugout canoe," Mutt whispered.

The canoe was mostly filled with forest duff, the result of nature's ongoing process of composting fallen leaves and debris. Within the canoe, a row of huckleberry bushes seemed to have taken root, as if replacing its original occupants.

Carved from a massive cedar log, the dugout canoe bore faint yet unmistakable axe marks on its sides and tapered front. It measured about three feet wide and fifteen feet long.

We began removing the forest duff and huckleberry bushes from the canoe, revealing a relic of Native American history. How long had this canoe been resting here? Given that this discovery took place in the mid-1950s, it was possible that its last passengers navigated these waters within the previous fifty to seventy-five years. It could even have been undisturbed for a century or more.

We tried pulling the canoe from the water but quickly realized it was firmly entrenched in the peat bog and locked in the mysteries of history.

Excitement about our discovery was hard to contain at the supper table that evening. And for the exclusive benefit of Odin, we decided to start the conversation with …

"There's a boat at Holms Lake."

Stephen and Sharon pose with Dave's 1938 International truck.

—— ·•· ——

CHAPTER 16

EDUCATORS

O din looked at me, expecting an answer. Another trick question I would try to ignore. "Did you ever wonder why, after you cut down a tree, it is no longer a tree?"

Pa, Dave, and Odin had been working for a couple of weeks harvesting massive Douglas fir trees from the woods behind the barn. These trees were cut down using a two-man crosscut saw, often referred to as a misery whip. In the 1950s, the gas-powered chainsaw was beginning to replace the crosscut saw in most logging operations, but our low-budget operation still depended on the misery whip. The logs were dragged out of the woods by a chain attached to the Farmall tractor, then loaded onto Dave's 1938 International flatbed truck by means of a ramp. This was a poor man's logging operation. The income from the sale of these logs would be small, but a needed boost to the family income.

"Did ya hear my question?" Odin was persistent.

"What are ya talking about?"

I was annoyed by the question but gave the answer I was sure could not be challenged. "A tree is a tree when it's up and when it's cut down it's still a tree." I would be prepared to argue this point, even if Odin was eight years older.

"OK then," Odin replied. "What is that laying over there?"

"A log." I said timidly. My confidence was already fading.

Odin grinned, and then finished me off: "When a tree is standing, it is a tree. When it is cut down, it becomes a log. And when it is stood back up, it's a pole."

I walked away. I was wounded, but much smarter. This kind of education came in erratic spurts, often at the expense of my self-esteem. Conversely, Odin seemed to garner immense pleasure from these teaching moments. It's this kind of teaching that begins to mold a person's mind in quirky ways.

If my early home-grown education prepared me for formal education, it was not evident. First grade did not begin well. My first day at Lincoln Elementary School proved to be a disaster. Miss Atkins was an energetic teacher, but I found her to be woefully lacking in basic knowledge. Burn Hill folk don't cave in to forced indoctrination, so my conflict with Miss Atkins occurred before recess on the first day. My skeptical little mind began to stiffen when I was told that a rabbit was actually a child that could read fast and well. I found it equally hard to accept a doctrine that implied that a turtle was a hapless child who read slowly and could only read a few words in a Dick and Jane book.

Dick and Jane—even the names of the title characters can put one to sleep. The hard-bound classic was the standard "learn to read" book employed by well-meaning teachers across America. As boring as this book certainly was, there were some kids who actually learned to read it. These were for the most part kids that were not raised on Burn Hill, and who had not experienced any greater excitement than the simplistic stories found in the book.

Miss Atkins said I could become a rabbit if I worked really hard. The other kids seemed to rejoice at this kind of fanciful hogwash, but I soundly rejected it. Pa worked really hard, and he hadn't turned into a rabbit. Already I did not like school. I would tell Ma about this crazy teacher when I got home.

At recess I thought about being a turtle. I didn't like turtles. I sat over against a big maple tree in the schoolyard and watched the rabbits and the turtles jumping rope and playing tag. Most of the rabbits were pathetically slow and awkward. They couldn't jump rope and were easily tagged out by the faster turtles. I planned to join the recess activities, but for now I was satisfied to stay by the maple tree and evaluate this zoo.

There had been talk at home, even before my first day of school, that Miss Atkins was young and pretty. At six years of age, I could distinguish between young and old, but had not yet developed an awareness of cute or ugly. While the rabbits and the turtles played, Miss Atkins and the second-grade teacher, Mrs. Simpson, patrolled the playground. I watched these two and began to understand the complexities of attractiveness. It was an exercise of stare and compare.

It was the first time in my life I had even thought about comparing one woman with another. Miss Atkins was easy to look at. She had a slim build, about just right, I figured. She had smooth skin and well-styled blond hair. Her dress fit.

Mrs. Simpson was not so easy to look at. She was shorter than Miss Atkins and much wider. Her hair amounted to two bunched-up humps on the top of her head, a mass of fuzzy disorder that reminded me of two roosters in a fight. I preferred to look at Miss Atkins, but in order to fully educate myself on the topic, I continued to study Mrs. Simpson. Her dress did not fit; and it was not just a matter of fit, for there was a profound lumpiness to her anatomy that no seamstress could disguise. I immediately thought of a gunnysack filled with pumpkins. The two walked slowly past my station at the big maple tree. Mrs. Simpson's legs were skinny, unlike the upper portion of her anatomy. Her elbows were skinny too, but above and below her elbows her arms were heavy and wobbled in a way that seemed to affect her equilibrium. It was a horrific sight.

"Are you OK?" Mrs. Simpson was looking at me. Am I OK? I thought to myself. Had Mrs. Simpson never looked into a mirror? There were a few things she needed to attend to before asking me if I was OK, beginning with the two roosters still going at it on top of her head.

"Are you OK?"

Yes, I was OK, but I needed a moment to get my thoughts reorganized.

"Oh, he's one of my little turtles." Miss Atkins smiled sweetly.

The bell rang. Recess was over. I followed Miss Atkins back to the classroom.

"Welcome back, my little rabbits and turtles." I decided she was prettier patrolling the playground.

I had a name tag that was attached to my shirt with a safety pin. I was pretty sure it said turtle, because when Miss Atkins said, "OK, I want all my little turtles to sit over in the corner on the floor" she motioned me into the corner.

So, I was a turtle? I was not happy and decided to put on a pouty face for the rest of the day. I could accept being called Cramp at home, but turtle?

"Now open your readers." Readers, what kind of crazy talk is this? I sat on the floor holding what most people would recognize as a book.

"Open your reader, Andrew," Miss Atkins said, reaching down and opening my book to page one. So, a book is a "reader," I surmised. I did not like school.

"I will read," she said. She pointed to each word as she read.

"Looooooook looooooook.

Ooooooooh, ooooooooh, ooooooh.

Looooooook, looooooook.

Ooooooooh, looooooook."

Did Miss Atkins have to point to each word? I was not impressed with this "reader" thing.

"Let's try another page" she said.

"Seeeeee Jaaaaaaane ruuuuuuun.

Seeeeeee Jaaaaaaane ruuuuuuun."

She sounded ridiculous. Why doesn't she just read like the rabbits?

"Now you read it, Andrew." I was annoyed and could see no sense in taking all day to read three words, so I marched the three words off my tongue in rapid fire: "See Jane run."

She waited, then pointed to the page. "Don't stop; keep reading. Read the second line."

Why would I want to repeat myself? "See Jane run" I said, even faster.

Now she was annoyed.

It took all day for the turtles to get through four pages of the most pathetic book I had ever seen. In the other corner the rabbits were rapidly chewing through their book and seemed to be enjoying every bite. It was sickening.

If one is to accept the premise that school is a place where adults transmit their accumulated knowledge to the next generation, then we had a real problem at Lincoln Elementary. And to think that I was attending a school named after Abraham Lincoln. Wasn't he the kid who never went to school, who just opened a Bible one day and started to read?

"In the beginning God created the heaven and the earth. And the earth was without form and void; and darkness was upon the face of the deep."

I was pretty sure Mr. Lincoln would not think much of the Dick and Jane book, or a school that divided kids into groups of turtles and rabbits.

After my first day had mercifully come to an end, Ma came to school to pick me up. I believe she wanted to talk with Miss Atkins. Given my aggressive approach to life, she may have had misgivings about my ability to fit into a structured class environment. Ma talked quietly with Miss Atkins, while I waited near the door. I could not hear much of the conversation, but I did hear Miss Atkins say, "Had Andrew attended kindergarten last year, I'm sure he would have advanced to become a rabbit by now." Even Ma appeared puzzled by the statement.

My educational experiences extended beyond the homegrown wisdom of Burn Hill and the challenging methods of Lincoln Elementary. To round out my education, I was taken to church three or four times a week. At a young age, even before I became a turtle, I grasped that a church was not merely a building, but rather a gathering of like-minded individuals. This theological concept was preached with conviction by stern-faced men of the pulpit. It was also considered proper to refer to the gathering as the "assembly" rather than using the word "church," a point that perplexed the average person.

The church building we frequented was situated just off Main Street in downtown Arlington. The big, boxy white structure boasted a simple design. In its earlier years, the building had belonged to another church organization, and under that ownership it had a grander appearance that included a steeple. After acquiring this building, the assembly leaders decided to remove the steeple, making it less reminiscent of a traditional church building. While this act of reverse construction may have confused the average person, it was deemed a necessary step. Our church leaders often pointed out that the building should not be the focal point of the assembly.

No services were held in the big white building; or at least the gatherings were never referred to as services. One might attend a prayer meeting, but not a prayer service. The distinction was that prayer services took place in churches, while prayer meetings were held in the assembly. I doubt the average person was even aware of this distinction, and their ignorance likely spared them from going insane.

During these meetings, profound silence filled the room. Apart from the voices of men preaching or praying, or the singing of hymns, the only sounds were the creaking of pews, a fussing infant, the occasional cough, or the faint growling of hungry stomachs. These bodily noises were a challenge to control and often embarrassed those who emitted them.

In Sunday school, Miss Carrie Terhorst taught me to read words from the Bible that only a Scrabble expert could appreciate. Words like "escheweth," "unction," and "holpen" intrigued me and stuck in my mind, even though I didn't fully understand their meanings. Surprisingly, I haven't had the opportunity to use these words in speech or writing until now.

It was the assembly brethren who taught me to pray using seventeenth-century English. It was considered disrespectful to use modern personal pronouns when addressing God in prayer. A proper and reverent prayer required the use of archaic pronouns such as "Thee," "Thou," "Thy," and "Thine." Attaching the proper verb to these personal pronouns was even more challenging, requiring phrases such as "Thou art," "Thou wert," "Thou wast," "Thou hast," "Thou wouldst," "Thou doest," "Thou wilt," and "Thou knowest."

For a young learner of this challenging language, utilizing it felt awkward. Not only did I have to learn the old English personal pronouns and associated verbs, but there was also an array of other antiquated words and phrases that were part of the language of prayer.

A properly constructed prayer, to a person well practiced, would go something like this: "Thou hast gathered us together to seek Thy face in humble prayer. We come with contrite hearts, knowing that Thou art an omniscient God of unwavering holiness. As we have assembled thus at Thy behest, we rest in Thy gracious and benevolent hands. And under the cover of Thy wings, Thou hast provided solace to our weary souls."

Mastering this language was a challenge, but if one hoped to be proficient in prayer, this style of speech had to be learned. Uttering a prayer in modern English, no matter how sincere the intentions, was considered disrespectful and a grave offense.

Despite the barriers presented by seventeenth-century English in prayer, I learned the fundamental truths about God and myself—firstly, that God loved me like no other, and secondly, that I needed reconciliation with Him. Reconciliation was made possible because Jesus Christ, God's Son, died to cancel my personal debt of sin. On May 20, 1956, at the age of ten, I placed my faith in Jesus Christ. The peace and joy I found on that day continue to this day and will only grow as eternity unfolds before me.

Every man and boy old enough to sit upright in a pew was expected to wear pressed pants and a jacket, a white button-up shirt, and a necktie. Dressing in this manner was seen as a way to show respect for God and the dignity of the occasion. Women had more options for attire, as long as it was modest.

There was one clothing peculiarity that puzzled me—some ladies wore furry objects to the meetings. When I whispered to Ma about the furry thing draped on Mrs. Colburn's shoulders, Ma whispered back, "It's a mink stole."

"She stole it?" I asked.

Ma quickly covered my mouth with her hand, giving me a stern look. "Shush— we'll talk about it when we get home."

In the meantime, I kept an eye on these stolen creatures adorning Mrs. Colburn's neck. To my five-year-old eyes, those animals appeared very much alive. The mink still had their pointy heads with black beady eyes, complete with tiny little feet and toes. I studied those four creatures intently throughout the one-hour meeting.

I wasn't convinced those furry little mammals were dead; perhaps they were only wounded. They seemed to move a bit on Mrs. Colburn's shoulders, especially when hymns were sung.

I looked at Ma, signaling that I had more questions, but she raised a finger, indicating that further inquiries were not welcome.

At home, I received a full education about mink stoles. Pa joined in the discussion.

The mink stole I had observed at the meeting consisted of four complete animals, devoid of their original organic stuffing and bones. The model Mrs. Colburn was wearing was simply four of these long, skinny creatures sewn together, nose to back feet, nose to back feet, with the tails left to dangle. The four mink formed an open square, with each mink in a kind of track race around her neck. To wear one of these peculiar accessories, a lady would slip her head through the open square, allowing the four mink to drape over her shoulders.

"They're quite expensive," Ma explained.

"Is that why she stole it?" I asked innocently.

"No, she didn't steal it. She probably inherited it from her mother."

"Do you have one, Ma?" I couldn't resist asking.

Ma shook her head. "Good," I said. "You don't need one."

I was relieved to learn that Mrs. Colburn had acquired the mink stole honestly. I liked Mrs. Colburn, and I also liked her cute daughter, Virginia (aka Ginger), who was three weeks older than me. Marriage wasn't on my mind at that time, but fifteen years later, it certainly was. In 1966, I married that cute girl, and the seventeenth-century English I learned from the assembly brethren came in handy when I repeated the words "I plight thee my troth."

Dave proudly poses on the 1938 Farmall F-12, that he and Odin
purchased with their own hard-earned money. This tractor proved
invaluable on the farm. Plowing, discing, cutting and raking hay, logging
and joy riding were all within the capabilities of this work horse.

CHAPTER 17

MOVING ON

This day was inevitable. As much as life on Burn Hill was an extraordinary and unique experience, it had to come to an end. The meager wage of just over a dollar per hour that Pa earned at Acme Box and Veneer couldn't sustain the family any longer. By 1958, Dave and Odin had already left home in search of better opportunities, receiving technical training and finding employment in Tacoma and Seattle. For the Hale family to continue living a primitive lifestyle on Burn Hill wouldn't provide the remaining kids with a clear vision of the future or motivate them to strive for something better.

Perhaps the primary motivation for Pa to initiate the move was to give Ma a more comfortable and modern lifestyle. Throughout the 1950s, Pa had made various improvements to the old Burn Hill house, but there was still no indoor bathroom. The toilet remained a rickety outhouse perched over a smelly pit, and baths were still taken in a galvanized wash tub on the kitchen floor. The well would run dry in the summer, necessitating weekly trips to town to fill a water tank in the family pickup truck. At this point in Pa and Ma's lives, they had very little to show for their struggles except for a well-functioning family. However, the challenge of moving on from Burn Hill would be significant.

Pa, whose full name was Donald Eugene Hale, was born in 1913 into a middle-class family in Iowa. His father was a postmaster and small business owner in the town of Tripoli. With the Great Depression paralyzing the country in 1929 and Pa graduating from high school in 1930, there were limited opportunities for a bright future. To compound the bleak economic conditions, Pa's father lost his position as postmaster. In 1934, Pa left Iowa and rode west on his Harley-Davidson motorcycle in search of a better life. By the grace of God, he met Dorothy McDougall, a beautiful and petite young lady, the daughter of an apple grower in Wenatchee, Washington. Ma, whose full name was Dorothy Priscilla McDougall, was also from the Midwest. She was born in 1912 into a farming family in Wabasso, Minnesota, and moved with her family to Washington State when she was twelve.

Pa and Ma were married in 1935. They moved to Granite Falls, Washington, in 1939 and then to Arlington in 1943. On March 17, 1945, they moved to Burn Hill. During those years, Pa worked several low-paying jobs, including being a dry cleaner deliveryman, service station attendant, farmhand, store clerk, and dairy deliveryman.

By the mid-1950s, Pa was still working a low-paying job operating a wood slicing machine at Acme Box and Veneer. Recognizing the need for change, Pa decided to learn electronics, realizing his need to acquire a marketable skill. In the spring of 1958, at the age of forty-four, Pa enrolled in a correspondence course offered by National Technical Schools in Los Angeles, California. This study program in Radio, Television, and Allied Electronics was similar to modern-day online university courses, but without the aid of a computer. Written study materials were sent to Pa through the mail, and upon completion of his studies, he would take written exams. The exams were then mailed back to California for grading. Pa excelled in this course, acing all of his exams. He had a brilliant mind and a history of being an exceptional student, having skipped a grade level in high school and graduating at the age of seventeen. The correspondence course became Pa's golden ticket to a brighter future for the Hale family. In the summer of 1958, while continuing with the correspondence course, Pa was hired at Boeing Company as an electrical planner.

On August 14, 1958, Pa placed the following advertisement in the Arlington Times newspaper:

FOR SALE – 4 Bedroom home, 10 acres

Partially cleared, Barn for 2 cows, Orchard, Tractor

$7,000. Terms. Don Hale, Rt 2, Phone 309

Moving day arrived in the fall of 1958. I had completed one quarter of my seventh grade when the Burn Hill farm was sold. The impending move created excitement for some members of the family, but for me it was a source of dread. I considered myself a country boy, and Burn Hill was my proud country haven. Our family used the term "city slicker" to refer to people who lived in the city. I was never told the exact meaning of "city slicker," but it didn't sound good, and I wanted no part of it. For a twelve-year-old kid like me, life on Burn Hill was everything I wanted. There was ample room to roam and the freedom to do so. Vast acres of forest awaited exploration, with trees to climb, grassy fields to frolic in, and a meandering creek. The big barn provided a perfect hideout on rainy days. There was a variety of farm animals and a large Farmall tractor I could drive almost anytime I wished. I didn't know much about city life, but I knew that all of this would soon be left behind.

We rented a moving truck and packed our belongings, leaving behind anything associated with country living. The buyer of the property would inherit the Farmall tractor and the 1940 Ford pickup truck that I had hoped would be mine someday. Ma was more than happy to leave behind anything that hinted at primitive living. Wash tubs, clotheslines, barn boots, and kerosene lamps were abandoned.

The route to our new home south of Seattle followed Highway 99. At that time, Interstate 5 had not yet been constructed. Highway 99 was the only option available, requiring navigating through the downtown streets of Everett and Seattle. Dave was designated as the driver of the rented truck, and I was the lucky kid who got to ride in the cab with him. Queenie, our dog, wasn't accustomed to riding in a vehicle but eventually settled down at my feet. Pa drove the family car with Ma and the rest of the kids.

Having a new home with a bathroom felt like a remarkable luxury. That night, I soaked in a shiny white bathtub, amazed at its size and the ample space to stretch out and relax. After having to curl up in a three-foot-diameter galvanized wash tub for the first twelve years of my life, this was an incredible upgrade. If there were any upsides to this city living, a bathtub and an indoor toilet were certainly among them. That night, there was a lineup to try out the toilet and to luxuriate in a real bathtub.

There were many adjustments for everyone with this new city lifestyle. For Ma, the move was a well-deserved upgrade, providing a comfortable home with most of the modern amenities expected in the late 1950s. The small, fenced backyard posed a more challenging and distasteful experience for Queenie. Being a country dog, she was used to roaming in wide-open spaces without the confinement of a fence. The adjustments were equally difficult for us kids. We were the new kids on the block and had to find our way in this unfamiliar environment. There was a new school, new friends, and a new church.

With this new beginning, the bizarre nicknames that Dave and Odin had assigned to every sibling younger than themselves faded from use. I was happy to say goodbye to "Cramp," and gladly went by "Andy." Pa and Ma never bought into nicknames in the first place, and to them I would always be "Andrew." Annie Oakly had faded from use even before we left Burn Hill. She was "Priscilla," and if the occasion called for a less formal name, she was "Cill." Marilyn was more than happy to leave "Mutt" back in the weeds of Burn Hill. Reuben lost the nickname "Batis," Stephen lost "Dez," and was now "Steve." And lastly, Sharon outgrew the nickname "Bits."

In retrospect, this move was the right decision for the family. At the time, I was too young to fully grasp the effort Pa made to lift his family out of poverty. Pa's job at Boeing provided a livable wage to support the family, and he found fulfillment in his new job, which he truly loved.

In February 1961, Pa received his diploma from National Technical Schools. Ma's life became easier, allowing her more time to engage in activities she loved, such as sewing, knitting, and gardening. Surprisingly, us kids were doing okay too, finding our way in a strange new world and adapting to a faster-paced urban lifestyle.

After Pa retired from Boeing in 1978, he and Ma enjoyed a more relaxed lifestyle. They both reveled in gardening and spent time together tending to a large vegetable and flower garden. They purchased a pickup truck with a camper unit and relished in their travels. They cherished family, and whenever the family gathered, Pa and Ma were content to sit back and listen to the kids recount stories of Burn Hill. Pa was the ultimate handyman and craftsman, always eager to help family members with projects. The needs of the church were forever close to their hearts, and they continued to contribute in numerous ways. After leading lives of exemplary and faithful service, Pa and Ma went home to Heaven to receive their reward, with Ma passing away in 1985 and Pa joining her in 1997.

Many years have passed since the Hale family moved on from Burn Hill. We have physically departed from that cherished piece of land, but emotionally and spiritually, there remains an unbreakable connection. Pa and Ma's consistent and godly lives spoke powerfully to each of the eight kids. The message of the Bible and the saving grace of God resulted in all eight kids trusting Jesus Christ as their Savior and Lord.

The value of Burn Hill cannot be measured by any conventional metric but by the quality of the people who lived and grew from it. The family that emerged from Burn Hill learned that a lack of possessions does not equate to poverty, a lack of education does not mean ignorance, a lack of status does not imply insignificance, a lack of culture does not equate to failure, and a lack of resources does not signify a lack of opportunity.

Burn Hill provided an experience that was free, but it should have cost millions.

Hale siblings gather in 2013 to tell and retell the stories of Burn Hill.
Dave, Odin, Priscilla, Marilyn, Andrew, Reuben, Stephen, Sharon.

Ma and Pa in retirement. A life well lived, a reward
well deserved, a memory most cherished.

EIGHT KIDS AFTER BURN HILL

D ave Hale left Burn Hill in 1956 to attend Tacoma Technical and Vocational School for a course in welding and diesel and heavy equipment. During this time, Dave worked for Concrete Technology Company as a welder for steel used in pre-stressed concrete. In 1957, Dave was hired by Boeing Company as a structural aircraft mechanic on airplane models B-52 and 707. Dave married Donna Miller in 1957. He was drafted into the US Army in 1959, and went through boot camp at Fort Ord, California. Dave trained as an army medic, and Donna joined him as he was stationed in San Antonio, Texas, and Louisville, Kentucky, and a US Army base in Wildflecken, Germany. Dave was the consummate soldier and excelled in military culture, attaining the rank of Sergeant E5 in just two years. Dave and Donna had three children, Janice, Jonathan, and Jason. Dave was hired at Sears, Roebuck and Company in 1964, first as a store clerk, then advancing to become a regional sales manager. Dave and Donna lived in Seattle, Normandy Park, and North Bend, Washington. Dave retired in 1992, after a twenty-eight-year career with Sears. Always the one who was willing to take on responsibility, he retired at the early age of fifty-six to be the loving caregiver for Pa, who needed daily care following a stroke. Dave went home to be with the Lord on July 22, 2021.

Odin Hale enlisted in the US Navy when he was nineteen. After completing boot camp in 1958, he married Arlene Ryburg, and they had two children, Irene and Charlotte. Their first home was San Diego, where Odin studied electronics, graduating first in his class. He was assigned to missile research and development at White Sands Missile Range and aboard guided missile cruiser Galveston. Odin and Arlene lived in El Paso, Texas; Norfolk, Virginia; Paulsboro, New Jersey; and Philadelphia. In 1962 they moved to Seattle, and Odin was hired by Boeing Company to work in Minuteman missile testing and satellite prototype electronics development. In 1964, Odin began a civil service career based at Naval Torpedo Station in Keyport, Washington. Odin and Arlene lived in Seattle, Bainbridge Island, and Bremerton, Washington; San Diego, California; and Nanaimo, BC, Canada. As an electronics technician, Odin soon advanced to combat systems specialist while directing anti-submarine warfare testing of submarines and destroyers. In 1977, Odin was promoted to range manager of the Joint Canadian/US Navy Undersea Test Range, Nanoose Bay, BC, Canada. Odin accepted early federal retirement in 1988 and they returned to the U.S. in 1996 for full-time care of Arlene's mother. Odin and Arlene are currently living in the Ballard district of Seattle, Washington.

Priscilla Hale Thurber, aka Annie Oakley: As soon as Priscilla graduated from Arlington High School in 1958, she accepted a medical technology internship at Swedish Hospital in Seattle, graduating with a National Registration Diploma in 1960. Priscilla married in 1960, and had two children, Carol and Brian. Priscilla's career spanned a period of fifty-three years, in which she held positions in several major Seattle hospitals, including histologist, histology supervisor, pathology transcriptionist, manager of neuropathology, clinical research, and clinical histology. Priscilla helped develop a laboratory discipline called Flow Cytometry DNA Analysis. Priscilla enjoyed teaching clinicians and researchers from around the world, and traveled to histology conventions and International Society for Advancement of Cytometry conferences throughout the world. She also traveled to far-away destinations to teach in France, England, Greece, Denmark, Estonia, Russia, and Vietnam. Priscilla retired in 2005, and is currently living in Edmonds, Washington.

Marilyn Gratias, aka Mutt, was fourteen years old at the time of our move to Seattle. After graduating from high school, she worked for one year as a nanny to two young children. In 1964, Highline Community College offered a new two-year RN program, the first of its kind in the area. Out of two hundred applicants, Marilyn was one of only twenty-five who were selected for acceptance into this highly competitive program. After graduating and passing state boards, she worked as a registered nurse in Labor and Delivery at West Seattle General Hospital. Marilyn married Don Gratias in 1967, after Don completed basic training in the US Army. Marilyn and Don lived in San Antonio, Texas, while Don received training as a combat medic, then spent eighteen months together in Frankfurt, Germany, where Don completed his military obligation. Marilyn and Don have three children, Jeffrey, Aaron, and Tamara. In 1969 Marilyn and Don moved to Grants Pass, Oregon, where they helped establish a Christian church, and where Marilyn has been a life-long Sunday school teacher. Marilyn worked for several years as a special education teacher's aide, teaching children with learning disabilities. Her other jobs included customer service clerk in the family-owned print shop, set-up technician/checker at Walmart, clerk at a Bible Book Store, and eight years as a caregiver to an Alzheimer patient. Marilyn and Don are currently living in Grants Pass, Oregon.

Andrew Hale, aka Cramp: I was twelve years old when we moved from Burn Hill to Seattle. After graduating from high school, I was hired by Boeing Company in 1965. I worked as a template and tooling maker, and then continued as a technical illustrator and graphic artist. In 1966 I married Virginia Colburn, a young lady I had known since toddlerhood, who grew up on a dairy farm just three miles from our Burn Hill home. We had two children, Cheryl and Justin. In 1969 to 1970, Boeing laid off 34,700 employees in what was known as the Boeing Bust. I was laid off in 1970. I worked at gardening jobs for the next two years, then in 1972 I started Hale Company Inc., a landscape design, installation, and maintenance company. That same year I received certification as a MASTER GARDENER from Washington State University. I sold the company in 2015. I continue to do landscape design and consulting. In 2016, my son Justin and I established Pre64Win Inc., an online company in the business of buying, selling, and restoring vintage Winchester rifles, including custom rifles built in our Woodinville shop. Virginia and I have lived in Burien, North Seattle, and Bothell, Washington, and currently live in Woodinville, Washington.

Reuben Hale, aka Batis, was nine years old when the family left Burn Hill. The new Hale home was in the Burien area of Seattle. After graduating from high school in 1967, Reuben attended Seattle Pacific College for one quarter, before dropping out and going to work as an engineering aid at Boeing Company. Reuben married Lois Portman in 1969 and they made their home in North Seattle. In that same year, Reuben decided the engineering world was not for him, so he left Boeing to purchase a landscape gardening business. Reuben and Lois had three children, Douglas, Sheila, and Lauren. Reuben operated Hale's Gardening in Seattle until the year 2000, when he and Lois moved to Omak, Washington. There, Reuben started another gardening business, High Place Environmental. Reuben and Lois also worked together, buying, remodeling, and renting three homes in the Omak area. Reuben purchased 120 acres with a lake seven miles south of Okanogan in the Colville Reservation in Washington. There he built a beautiful get-away cabin overlooking the lake. Reuben retired in 2019. Reuben and Lois are currently living in Omak Washington.

Stephen Hale, aka Dezeets, was seven years old at the time the Hale family moved to Seattle. Following graduation from high school in 1969, Steve attended Renton Vocational Technical Institute in automotive mechanics. Steve married Margaret Hutchison of Vancouver, BC, in August 1971. Steve worked for Frank Kenney Toyota in Seattle until 1976. During this time, Steve and Margaret lived in Tukwila, Seattle, and Alderwood Manor, Washington. Steve and Margaret had four children, JoAnne, Marilyn, Elizabeth, and Robert. In 1976, Steve began working for Metro Transit in Seattle as a heavy diesel mechanic. In 1981, Steve and Margaret purchased 2.5 acres of land in Snohomish and built a log home. In 1994 they moved to Chesaw, Washington, buying 163 acres of land and placing a new manufactured home on the property. Here Steve and Margaret enjoyed ranch-style living. Steve worked for Okanogan Farm Equipment in Okanogan, Washington, until 1996, when a serious car accident left Steve unable to work for a long period of time. Steve and Margaret moved to Tucson, Arizona, in 2006, where Steve worked for a generator service company until 2007. Steve worked at SunTran Transit in Tucson as a mechanic from 2007 to 2011, at which time he retired. Stephen and Margaret are currently living in Vail, Arizona.

Sharon Hale Mclaughlin, aka Bits, was six years old when the family left Burn Hill. After high school, Sharon received training at Harborview Hospital and received certification as a histotechnician by the American Society for Clinical Pathology. Sharon married in 1975, and had two children, Ryan and Michael. Sharon worked in several hospital labs, including the University of Washington, BC General Hospital, Harborview Medical Center, and Fred Hutchinson Cancer Research Center. Sharon's forty-seven-year career provided a wide range of experience, involving research, processing clinical surgical specimens, and working alongside a dentist in the development of the titanium implant. During her career as a histotechnician, Sharon advanced the ability of pathologists to identify additional tissue components. She was credited for the development of numerous special stain procedures to assist in cancer diagnosis. In 2016, Sharon was invited to Washington, DC, to present before the National Histology Society. Sharon lived in both Vancouver, BC, and Seattle. Sharon retired in 2018 and currently lives in Ocean Shores, Washington.

Andy and Virgina in 2016 celebrating 50 years
of marriage at Machu Picchu, Peru.